WORDS
FOR
WARRIORS

Other Books by Sam Sorbo

Gizmoe: The Legendary Journeys: Auckland

They're YOUR Kids

Teach from Love

Let There Be Light

Share the Light

True Faith: Embracing Adversity to Live in God's Light

WORDS
FOR
WARRIORS

Fight Back Against Crazy Socialists
and the Toxic Liberal Left

SAM SORBO

Humanix Books
www.humanixbooks.com

Humanix Books
Words for Warriors
Copyright © 2021 by Sam Sorbo
All rights reserved.

Humanix Books, P.O. Box 20989, West Palm Beach, FL 33416, USA
www.humanixbooks.com | info@humanixbooks.com

Humanix Books is a division of Humanix Publishing, LLC. Its trademark, consisting of the words "Humanix Books," is registered in the Patent and Trademark Office and in other countries.

Author photo by Natalia Melnikova.
Author illustration by Gilang Prima Sejati.

ISBN: 978-1-63006-185-2 (Hardcover)
ISBN: 978-1-63006-18-9 (E-book)

Printed in the United States of America
10 9 8 7 6 5 4 3 2 1

This book is dedicated to the Word.

Contents

D 49

Dark horse • Deficit • Delegate • Demagogue • Democracy • Deplorable • Ditto/Mega dittos/DittoHead • Drain the swamp • Dystopia

E 57

Economy • Education • Electorate • Emotional support animal • Environment (Environmentalist) • Equality • Euphemism • Executive branch

F 67

Face diaper • Fake news • Fascism • Feargasm • Filibuster • First Amendment • Fourth Amendment • Fredocon • Freedom • Front burner

G 77

Gaslighting • GDP/GNP • Genderbread person • Globalization • Global cooling • Global warming • Gosnell, Kermit • Grassroots • Green New Deal • Greenhouse effect • Grooming • Groupthink • Gubernatorial • Gun control

H 93

Habeas corpus • Happy warrior • Hegemony • House of Representatives • Humanism • Humble brag • Hypocrite

I 101

Ideology • Idiot • Immigration • Imperialism • Incentive • Incumbent • Ineptocracy • Infidel • Islam • Insurgents • Internationalism • Irreligion • ISIS

J 115

Jingoism • Judaism • Judicial branch • Junta • Jus ad bellum

K 121

KAG • Karen • Keynesian economics • Kitchen cabinet • Kleptocracy • Kwanzaa

S 197

Safe seat • Second Amendment • Secretary of state • Secular humanism • Senate • Sequester • Separation of powers • Serfdom • Sexual preference • Sharia law • Shelter-in-place • Slate • Smoke-filled room • Social contract • Social engineering • Social Security • Socialism • Sortition • Speaker of the House • Statist • Stimulus • Straw man argument • Sunset clause • Swing voter • Syndicalism • Systemic racism

T 221

Tea Party • TERF • Terrorism • Theocracy • Think tank • Totalitarianism • Transportation Security Administration (TSA) • Trojan horse • Trump Day • Trump effect

U 229

Unemployment rate • UBI or universal basic income • Useful idiot (Nancy Pelosi) • Utilitarianism

V 233

Veteran • Vice president

W 235

War • Wealth • Weather underground • Whip • White privilege • Woke • Wonk

X 241

Xenophobia

Z 243

Zeitgeist

Introduction

In the beginning was the word.

—John 1:1

While driving my kids to class one fine Friday morning, something that, as homeschoolers, we did only once a week, I embarked on a discussion of wealth.

"How do you think wealth is created, children? Do you know?"

"Well, you have to get a job, first," Shane says from the back seat. He is fifteen and just starting to come into his own as a young man.

"That's a way to start to accumulate wealth, yes, but it isn't how wealth is generated, necessarily. Let me explain. Wealth comes from the transaction." I paused for dramatic effect.

"What do you mean, 'transaction?'"

"Thank you for asking. I mean that when you bought your iPad, with your money, that was a transaction. Mind you, it has to be freely given, like the free market. But you freely traded money for the iPad because, ideally speaking, the iPad is worth a lot more to you than that money was to you. It's a whole world of information and a very useful tool, *n'est-ce pas?*"

Octavia, twelve, riding shotgun, nods and waits.

"And the store took your money because . . . , why? They have a ton of those iPads, but the money means much more to them than holding onto their stock of iPads, right?"

She giggles. "Of course."

"Who's wealthier?"

Silence, as they think it through.

"Both of them!" Shane pipes up from behind us. "Both sides got what they wanted, so they are both, in a way, wealthier, right?"

"Exactly! It's like magic—but it has to be free. It can't be coerced, because then it doesn't work, because wealth is actually a very personal thing. Shane, you love your 3D printer, so with that, you feel really wealthy. But I wouldn't want one of those, so I would feel poor if I had that instead of, say, my laptop."

"Right! And I prefer having my art supplies than that printer, or a calculator, or pretty much anything else. And I spend a lot of the money I earn on those things, because they make me happy."

"Another great point, Tave, because money doesn't provide happiness, but the things you can *exchange* it for can certainly help." I smiled. I loved these long drives with my kids, even if I had to force the conversation from time to time. Kids are like puzzles that we, as parents, need to pour over for lengths of time to figure out.

"So, Tave, you asked me before why we need to go to class, because you say you don't really enjoy spending the time with the other kids."

"They're just kind of juvenile, and I'd rather be doing my artwork."

"I get that, but we go to seminar once a week for the *conversation*." We had joined a national cooperative homeschool group called Classical Conversations for the group dynamic and the classical style of education, which provides a conversational component to the study of literature, the arts, mathematics, and all the disciplines. We pursue the Socratic method, which is a form of argumentative dialogue between individuals in the quest for truth, understanding, and education. One of the primary focuses in a Socratic dialogue is the definition of terms.

"You can't just live in a bubble, by yourself. We trade thoughts on the books and what we are studying because it is in the free *exchange* that wealth is created. And, while we vaguely understand that wealth is sort of metaphysical, because it's personal to each individual, intelligence is as well. 'Knowledge,' they say, 'is power' (like wealth, incidentally), and so, to exchange knowledge and trade ideas in a transactional setting, like this class, is a way to build your . . . your *smarts* savings account."

"Mom." My kids think my puns are dumb. I don't really care. I think they're funny.

We engage in the free exchange of ideas—something we lovingly refer to as *freedom of speech*—in order to build upon the past and create even greater prosperity for the future, just as in the marketplace of goods and services. Only the intellectual marketplace is for *ideas*. The United States not only created the greatest manufacturing and industrial engine of the world, but also, through our uniquely refined patent system, we generated a secure exchange in which ideas could flourish while being protected, and people could freely trade thoughts and concepts, new philosophies and theories, so that anyone might be able to contribute if they were willing to engage in *thought*.

Now, we are engaged in a great civil war, testing whether that system shaping a free marketplace of thoughts should endure. On college campuses, particular speakers are banned, rejected by leftists, and courses taught by professors insist on a groupthink mentality that allows for no entertainment of ideas foreign to the ones already accepted. Of course, this is extraordinarily dangerous.

Take, for instance, the Left's insistence that global climate change is both human caused and dangerous to the survival of the planet and that anyone or any statistic that disagrees with those notions must be not only wrong but also ignored, nay, *silenced*. Evidence clearly shows that the climate has changed from what it has been in the past. What is it about today's global climate that is perfect and must be preserved at all cost? (And, by *all cost*, I'm referring to the tremendously destructive Green New Deal.)

But disagree at your own peril. Leftist ideologues have no tolerance for dissenting ideas.

The Left's insistence on shutting down discourse is a direct attack on prosperity. The Left hates *wealth*. It is only via the free exchange of research and scientific advancements that we have progressed through history. But the Left, and now that is a descriptor, too, for Democrats, rejects freedom of speech and freedom of ideas. Your ideas must conform, or you will be canceled.

We see this in the ridiculous discrimination and sham trial of Brett Kavanaugh, while Joe Biden's accuser, who is more reliable, more recent, and has several corroborating witnesses (to Dr. Blasey Ford's zero) is silenced by Democrats and the leftist media. They insist on the silent treatment for everything with which they disagree, which might be fine if they actually knew things or promoted facts. But they don't. They make things up and then defend them to the death, all while refusing to learn anything substantial, because it might upset the delicate balance they maintain between their lies and their desires.

They redefine words, replace concepts; heck, they even reworked our genders. So confused, they have to take apart the English language, reimagine definitions, and even come up with some brand new words for the crazy stuff they are thinking up these days.

There's a word for that: *insanity*. Look it up.

Well, with all the hatred and obfuscation spewing from ideologues, media, social justice warriors, and political hacks, I'm fed up. I'm tired of their games, so I'm calling BS on them. It's time to set the record straight, especially for the folks who are just trying to enjoy the lives the Lord gave them and want a few things explained in easy-to-understand prose.

This book is for you. Reject the spin on the alphabet cable networks and the nonsense from the political NPCs (see **NPC** for explanation). In this book, you'll find the unvarnished truth and some unpolished fun.

They've hijacked words, and then used them against us.

But we're gonna take 'em back.

Because our *words* are our *thoughts*, and our *thoughts* are our *prosperity*.

Sam Sorbo

I'm a former lefty, I understand how vicious these people are. I understand that they feel they have the right to control the sandbox, and I am trying to orchestrate media that isn't just out there to push the right-of-center libertarian narrative. I'm out there to destroy the false order, the false control that the left has in controlling the mainstream media in America.

—Andrew Breitbart, founder of *Breitbart News*

Aberration

Noun

An oddity, a deviation from the expected or normal course.

The United States of America is an aberration. Why? Because throughout the history of civilization, societies' control came through bloodlines or conquering territory and enslaving its inhabitants. They historically (and currently) have been driven by the human desire for power and executing any means (or people) necessary to achieve the goal. Self-serving evil interests of greed and power have been the norm. America was founded upon a fixed moral values system stemming from our Creator, who does not change. Human worth, objective right and wrong, and individual liberty have made America the most successful force for good in the world. It is the steadfast *principles*, not the ever-swaying interests of the wicked human heart, that are at the core of our aberration nation.

Abortion

Noun

Synonyms: murder, infanticide, child sacrifice

The purposeful termination of a pregnancy involving pills or surgical tools, usually within the first 28 weeks of a typical 40-week gestation period. In the United States, as well as six other countries, including China and North Korea, there are efforts to legalize "partial birth" abortion, wherein the baby (fetus) is dismembered on its way out of the womb. (See **Gosnell, Kermit** and **Planned Parenthood**.)

Pro-abortion advocates deceptively cloak their arguments in the words "choice," "autonomy," "right to privacy," and "reproductive health" and traffic in "what if" scenarios:

- What if the woman can't afford a baby?
- What if the woman was raped?
- What if the baby is deformed?

There is no answer to any of these questions that addresses the heart of the issue: the value of a human life.

The "choice" they make is to end a life. Their "right to privacy" is taking away the baby's right to life. Their "autonomy" over their own body infringes upon the autonomy of the baby's body. Prenatal vitamins, regular checkups, and ultrasounds illustrate reproductive health. Abortion can harm a woman's health and reproduces nothing.

The baby is not a *part* of the woman's body, as pro-abortionists would have us believe. Pregnant women have two hearts, two brains, two livers, two different types of DNA? That's not a human woman, that's an extraterrestrial alien in a science-fiction movie.

Their arguments are rhetorical gymnastics rooted in narcissism. The woman is God. Her feelings, plans, and convenience are all that matter. If the baby interferes with her life, she determines that it has no value and can be destroyed.

They are employing immoral and dangerous rationale. Infants can be inconvenient. Two-year-olds can be inconvenient. We, as individuals, do not get to determine value and worth based on another individual's convenience in our lives.

Did you know that Justin Bieber, Cher, Tim Tebow, Rep. Marlin Stutzman (R-IN), Pope John Paul II, Celine Dion, and Nick Cannon were all born to mothers who almost aborted them but chose not to?

#ProLife, #ProBaby

Abrogation

Noun

The concept that automatically replaces or overwrites an earlier statement or rule with any later, contradictory one.

In the Quran, the law of abrogation implies that all new laws supersede any prior conflicting ones. This allows a person to quote parts of the Quran to mean one thing, though that meaning may have been replaced by another law meaning exactly the opposite. Muhammad's Quran reportedly contains abrogated (*nasikh*) and abrogating (*mansookh*) verses in 71 suras (chapters)—out of 114—comprising 62.28 percent of all the suras of the Quran that have had verses changed, overruled, or deleted.

The Quran is unique among all the holy scriptures of other peoples because it is the *only* one that allows the god of Muhammad, Allah, to keep changing his mind regarding his alleged revelations to Muhammad. Some pundits argue that this shows Muhammad's Allah as bereft of foresight, with a fickle mind and incapable of assessing the weaknesses and strengths of Muhammad or his followers. This is, of course, a blasphemous characterization of any omniscient divinity!

Ad hominem

Adjective

In Latin, the phrase literally means "arguing against the person." It is a logical fallacy used to attack an opponent's personal traits instead of arguing the case. This typically appeals to emotions and prejudice at the cost of rational intellect and logic.

Ad hominem attacks are juvenile and vapid, and when blindly accepted at face value, people use them as a magical force to marginalize the opposition. And Senator Harry Reid is the grand wizard.

He did not like President George W. Bush's position on . . . everything. How he argued his critique of the president—to a group of teenagers, no less: "I think this guy is a loser." Way to set an example for our youth, Harry.

Harry's ad hominem attacks: Tea Partiers are "anarchists"; he "heard" Mitt Romney is a tax evader; the Koch Brothers are "un-American."

"Karl Rove and the Republicans are looking forward to a break-fast the day after the election. They are going to assemble 17 angry old white men for breakfast, some of them will slobber in their food, some will have scrambled eggs, some will have oatmeal, their teeth are gone. But these 17 angry old white men will say, 'Hey, we just bought America. Wasn't so bad. We still have a whole lot of money left.'"

Unsubstantiated claims and hateful rhetoric are used to stir anger and obfuscate truth (see **Alinksy, Saul**; Rule 12). It is not the tactic of a true statesman. It is the tactic of a manipulator.

For Alinsky's 12 rules and summaries, please see Appendix A.

Affirmative action

Noun

Government-approved discrimination. The practice of giving pref-erential treatment, particularly in upper academia, to minorities and women in an effort to compensate for the historical disadvantages felt by these groups.

Affirmative action discourages effort and encourages a reliance on skin color and body parts. Which is too bad, because often it's the lack of fairness that provides the incentive to gain knowledge, work hard, hurdle obstacles, and press on toward a better life.

There has never been, and will never be, a policy that can com-pletely level the playing field of life. However, today, no matter our color, gender, or station in life, we all have the opportunity to play.

#LetsAffirmTruth, #AffirmMeritocracy

Alinsky, Saul (1902–1972)

Person

The creator of modern community organization and author of *Rules for Radicals*, a book on subverting organized government and fomenting rebellions to produce chaos and disrupt the status quo—that being liberty, "In God We Trust," and "E Pluribus Unum. Alinsky claimed his book was for the "have-nots" to take power away from the "haves." But in reality, it is not intended for the masses, but rather it is an instructional manual for "organizers" on how to gain *power* over and *control* of the masses. He dedicated his book to the Devil.

Wouldn't the *Father of Lies* be proud to read:

> An organizer working in and for an open society is in an ideological dilemma to begin with, he does not have a fixed truth—truth to him is relative and changing; everything to him is relative and changing . . .

Or this charming bit of crooked calculation:

> The end is what you want, the means is how you get it. . . . The man of action views the issue of means and ends in pragmatic and strategic terms. He has no other problem; he thinks only of his actual resources and the possibilities of various choices of action. He asks of ends only whether they are achievable and worth the cost; of means, only whether they will work.
>
> —Saul Alinsky, *Rules for Radicals*, 1971

Hillary Clinton wrote her senior thesis on Alinsky's controversial tactics. For what should be obvious reasons, her thesis is sealed from public view (much like her secretary of state emails, which she personally deleted from her private server. For Clinton and Alinsky, the end, no matter how unethical or illegal, justifies the means—to power.

For Alinsky's 12 rules and summaries, please see Appendix A.

#HillaryPleaseNo2016

Altruism

Noun

The practice of performing good deeds for others despite lack of reward or personal gain.

People argue that altruism cannot actually exist; good deeds are their own reward. On an episode of *Friends* ("The One Where Phoebe Hates PBS"), Phoebe proves herself incapable of performing a good deed for its own sake, as she becomes happy with success for a good deed. Cynically, if it makes someone happy to serve in the soup kitchen, we can assert, fairly convincingly, that every action is ultimately self-serving.

> *If any civilization is to survive, it is the morality of altruism that men have to reject.*
>
> —Ayn Rand

Ayn Rand's *Atlas Shrugged* is an anthem to limited government and conservatism, but she rejected religion. This, of course, is a very cynical way to view the world.

Anarchy

Noun

A state of disorder caused by a lack of authority or purposeful disregard of order (See **Alinsky, Saul**).

True anarchy is the complete absence of law and government, which appeals to some men with shaved heads, wallet chains, and steel-toed black boots, but when push comes to shove, nobody really wants true anarchy, because the ones pushing that idea are the tyrants who will seize power the moment your back is turned and demand order.

Community organizers often target anarchy as their goal. Like the leaders of the French and Bolshevik revolutions, today's leftists stir up anger among the masses by claiming oppression, encouraging a victimhood mentality, and promoting class warfare. Once the kindling of resentment is laid and the accelerant of bitterness poured, they light the match and up rage the flames of fury.

The riots of the 1960s, and more recently Ferguson and Baltimore, are nirvana for community organizers like Saul Alinksy, Hillary Clinton, and Barack Obama. But chaos is unsustainable, so inevitably someone must seize the reigns in an attempt to restore order. That's when tyrants step in, promising to restore order (under a black boot) and redistribute wealth (at the point of a gun).

Liberty only exists in the presence of moral law, where our God-given freedoms are protected by *limited, checked* government. Anarchy removes the rule of all law and inevitably leads to *excessive* government.

#WakeUpAmerica, #tcot, #CrookedHillary

Antifa

Political movement

According to its own website, Antifa, "short for anti-fascist, is a broad, community-based movement composed of individuals organizing against racial and economic injustice." The colors and imagery on the website are strangely reminiscent of the Nazi movement, and the tactics Antifa employs at public gatherings are characterized by violent mobs and looting. Does it count if you denounce the very tactics you use? Seems more like hypocrisy, really. They stand in defiance of President Trump, without building any actual case as to why. The president tweeted on May 31, 2020, Antifa would be designated as a terrorist organization.

Their problem is that they only know what they claim to stand against, but not what they specifically fight for, so they just bring violence and chaos, without offering solutions (destruction and anarchy not being terrifically creative or uplifting).

The website states, "We are mobilizing to help support Comrades affected by the current crisis against them." Sure, but what *crisis*? That they are poor or feel underprivileged, angry, dissatisfied with their lives? Join the club! Their claim is that fascism is running the show—with zero evidence. And why use "Comrades" with a capital *C* on the site?

Antifa is nothing but another arm of the Communist Party, organizing to prevent conservatives from expressing truth and wreaking mayhem and violence on our streets as a way to overthrow our democratically elected government.

Article V Convention

Would-be historical event

A convention of at least two-thirds of the states seeking to amend the Constitution. Never has the Constitution been amended in this manner, but the provision for this approach is found in Article V:

> The Congress, whenever two thirds of both houses shall deem it necessary, shall propose amendments to this Constitution, or, on the application of the legislatures of two thirds of the several states, shall call a convention for proposing amendments, which, in either case, shall be valid to all intents and purposes, as part of this Constitution, when ratified by the legislatures of three fourths of the several states, or by conventions in three fourths thereof, as the one or the other mode of ratification may be proposed by the Congress; provided that no amendment which may be made prior to the year one thousand eight hundred and eight shall in any manner affect the first and fourth clauses in the ninth section of the first article; and that no state, without its consent, shall be deprived of its equal suffrage in the Senate.

To date, 34 state legislatures have applied and issued a call for a convention. However, this is a cumulative number, and over the years, some of the states have rescinded their application, and there is debate as to whether or not an application can be rescinded.

The call for a convention has recently gained momentum due to the desire for a balanced budget amendment and citizens' increasing concern that the federal government has overreached its constitutional boundaries.

#ConventionOfStates, #Article5

Autocracy

Noun; **autocratic**, *adjective*

A system of government where one person retains all power. Fascism, communism, theocracies, and military dictatorships can all be autocratic.

It doesn't take a genius to deduce that this is a bad idea. Absolute power in the hands of one person, or a handful of persons, leads to tyranny. Nazi Germany, Maoist China, Stalin's Russia, Castro's Cuba, Assad's Syria, Kim-Jong Un's North Korea, and so on.

The United States owns the greatest success story of breaking out from under the autocratic rule of King George. Over the last 240 years, we proved that a government of the people, by the people, and for the people is the best political system in the history of humanity, for the welfare of the individual and the society. How? Just look at the wealth and incredible progress made because of U.S. advances in business and technology, prosperity that has ameliorated the lives of people the world over. Autocracies be damned!

Autonomy

Noun

A community or person practicing successful self-governance:

- Politically, we desire our state and local governments to have autonomy so as to appropriately address indigenous (local) issues.
- Personally, we desire autonomy in making decisions that affect our bodies, families, careers, and relationships.

Here's where it gets tricky. In certain instances, an individual's rationalization of autonomy negatively impacts the liberty and safety of other individuals and society as a whole.

- Abortion (the life of the unborn)
- Drug use (legalization)
- Prostitution (legalization)
- Redefining marriage (affects children)

Regarding abortion Supreme Court Justice Ruth Bader Ginsburg said, "The state controlling a woman would mean denying her full autonomy and full equality." In her opinion, personal autonomy trumps all. But that rationale easily becomes a justification for a free-for-all, do-whatever-I-want mentality. It ignores the moral obligation of autonomous individuals to act *ethically* and *sacrificially* to further a principled and safe society. This is why John Adams said, "Our Constitution is made only for a moral and religious people."

Ironically, while Justice Ginsburg touted personal autonomy, she flouted state autonomy by supporting the *federal* rulings of *Roe v. Wade* and same-sex marriage. She objected to a state "controlling" a woman but saw no problem with the federal court controlling the state. Autonomy begins with the individual but does not end there, because the individual participates in society.

Bailout

Noun

The crony capitalist's euphemism for crony capitalism, because it sounds like a kindness, although it's really just a new tax on the citizen. Rescuing a business or economy in need of financial assistance precollapse or prebankruptcy.

The Obama administration handpicked companies to receive a *bailout* with the stimulus—over $800 billion—in his ill-conceived effort to stem the catastrophic economic implosion that precipitated the housing loan collapse of 2008.

The economic theory used to support the bailout stimulus is based on the work of British economist John Maynard Keynes (1883–1946). (See **Keynesian economics**.) Bailouts are intrinsically anti–free market.

In a capitalist system, Sylvia's Nail Salon either provides decent manicures at a reasonable price or Sylvia goes out of business because customers prefer the more professional Betty's Beauty instead. But (perhaps because Sylvia is the president's wife's cousin), when the government determines that Sylvia must stay in business (too big to fail), it uses taxpayer money to bail out Sylvia and her sketchy salon. Sylvia continues delivering messy manicures, and the better Betty's Beauty is encouraged to lower service expectations as well, making a double loss for the consumer. Government involvement is self-destruction, as it is the taxpayers who pay, through the bailout, for the goods or services they have already rejected in the free market. It is government coercion, using citizen-provided tools, to subvert that apparent will of the free-market-expressed will of the taxpayer.

Advocates argue that bailouts save jobs and inject money into the economy. This deceptive method may seem effective in the short term, but long term it is destructive. A bailout shifts resources from the much more productive private sector to the less productive government, which rarely gets good value for its spending and often "invests" in companies for political gain. (See **Cronyism/Crony capitalism**.) Here are a few of the companies that received bailout funding:

- Solyndra (a California solar company): $535 million; then ultimately laid off 1,100 workers and went bankrupt. Abound Solar: $400 million. Obama claimed it "will manufacture advanced solar panels at two new plants, creating more than 2,000 construction jobs and 1,500 permanent jobs." Two years later it went bankrupt and left its 37,000-square-foot facility with hazardous waste and contaminated water.
- Beacon Power: $43 million. Bankrupt.
- Chrysler: $10.7 billion. Has not repaid $1.2 billion.
- General Motors: $50.7 billion. Has not repaid $11.4 billion.

The government handing out money to failing companies is pure folly. If private investors, who have much more knowledge and much more to lose by investing, have already fled, it is a sure sign that the company is a stinker. If a mother gives her child an iPod for Christmas and he loses it, then gives him another for his birthday and he breaks it, is it okay for the father to rob their neighbor to buy the son another one? The government thinks so, because that is precisely what it does when it bails out an irresponsible, mismanaged company.

Success was an individual achievement; failure was a social problem.

—Michael Lewis, author, *The Big Short*

Ballot

Noun

The device used to cast one's vote, the method We the People use to be heard, supporting, opposing, or instituting change.

> *The ballot is stronger than the bullet.*
>
> —Abraham Lincoln

Ballots are often secret, to prevent undue pressure on, or persecution of, the voter. This argument carries weight when applied to private individuals. Some people argue for secret ballot voting in the Capitol to prevent coercion within political caucuses. However, secrecy inevitably leads to more coercion; congresspeople can be swayed by special interests while still publicly claiming to represent their constituents. They could vote "yes," claim they voted "no," and We the People would be none the wiser.

Open ballots hold our representatives accountable. Secret ballots are best reserved for private citizens.

> *It's not who votes that counts . . . it's who counts the votes!*
>
> —Anonymous

Bankruptcy

Noun

The process by which an individual or business who is unable to pay its debts petitions the court for relief; the condition resulting from debts outweighing income. Although some bankruptcies result not because of poor financial decisions (i.e., medical bills, unexpected downturn in markets, or technological changes), the bankruptcy procedures represent a form of communism, where the spoils go to the entity or recipients with the most sway on the court, but the burden is carried by the unfortunate. The U.S. debt-to-gross domestic product (GDP) has increased over the recent decades to 110 percent in 2020, leading people to call the nation bankrupt.

Benghazi

Noun

On September 11, 2012, after mounting unrest, a terrorist group attacked the U.S. Embassy in *Benghazi,* Libya. U.S. Ambassador Christopher Stevens was tortured and murdered, along with three others of his diplomatic mission: Sean Smith, Tyrone S. Woods, and Glen Doherty.

The Obama administration initially tried to downplay the event (President Obama joked that the deaths were "not optimal" with Jon Stewart on *The Daily Show*), blaming a little-known video, calling it "spontaneous," and winning the November presidential election, but the tragedy culminated in several investigations and congressional testimony, during which then Secretary of Defense Leon Panetta claimed, "There wasn't enough time" to send reinforcements to the Benghazi compound to protect U.S. personnel there. Of course, the first follow-up question should have been, "How did you know how long the attack would last?" but nobody did.

Most notably, Hillary Clinton, then secretary of state, when asked why the administration deliberately lied about the attack, remarked, "What difference, at this point, does it make?" She was solely responsible for security at the compound (or lack thereof). Numerous requests for additional officers after her decision to draw down the protective forces there went completely unheeded.

Eventually it was discovered that Clinton had kept a private, unsecured email server, destroyed 30,000 emails, and bleached computer files in order to protect her privacy and deny the American people their right to know what their government officials were actually doing. What business was she conducting? Theories abound!

#ClintonCash

Big government

Political term

An overbearing government system that interferes in the everyday activities of its constituents.

Government is the administration of public policy. Inevitably, the bigger it gets, the more controlling it becomes. It has reached into our educational system with Common Core, our healthcare system with the Affordable Care Act, our businesses with mandates to raise the minimum wage and corporate tax rates and impose expensive, stifling environmental regulations.

Leftists promote government like pharmaceutical companies promote new drugs. They paint a picture of smiling, multiethnic, same-sex couples frolicking through meadows with a subsidized health insurance card in one hand and a condom in the other and neighborhoods of fenceless, impeccably furnished houses inhabited by fast-food employees in new Priuses, all paid for by flipping two all-beef patties at 15-plus dollars an hour.

Unlike the drug companies, leftists are not required to reveal the vital safety information: the ugly side effects of their product.

Warning: Big government *may cause increased corruption, bloating constipation, and loss of freedom. Do not engage in thinking when taking. Societies under the influence of unleashed, unchecked, and unrestrained government have resulted in the deaths of millions of citizens. Consult the Declaration of Independence, Federalist Papers, and Constitution before swallowing.*

Big government must increase taxes to fund expansion, causing wealth producers to decrease hiring and production and increase prices. While the Left wickedly claims that *Big G* can take care of everyone, the individual relinquishes personal responsibility and accountability and active compassion for their fellow man. We the People lose Second Amendment rights, religious expression, incandescent light bulbs, and many other individual freedoms, like choosing to drink soda with a straw.

You can't be for big government, big taxes, and big bureaucracy and still be for the little guy.

—Ronald Reagan

The bigger the state, the smaller the citizen.

—Dennis Prager

I think, with Obama and the progressives, you've seen a massive expansion of big government, and it's all based on a moral premise. The moral premise is that wealth is theft. And I don't just mean the wealth of America, I mean, your wealth, my wealth.

—Dinesh D'Souza

A government big enough to give you everything you want is big enough to take away everything you have.

—Thomas Jefferson (attributed)

#BigGovernment, #Liberty

Bigot

Noun

A person who, unfairly or with ill-intent, judges another by some superficial quality such as the color of their skin or their accent.

Bigot has been mangled, distorted, and co-opted by those who abhor dissent (unless it's them dissenting) and used as a weapon to shut down legitimate debate on an issue:

- "It's unfair to the female students to allow boys who feel like girls to use the same locker room."
  Bigot.
- "I support traditional marriage, and here's why . . ."
  Homophobic bigot.

- "Illegal aliens . . ."
  The I word is hate speech, you racist bigot.

It's the retort du jour, typically accompanied by side dishes of lawsuits, job firings, threats, and destruction. (See also **Racist**.) What's absent from the menu is critical thinking and reasonable discourse. Check please!

President Obama campaigned on traditional marriage in 2008 and then "evolved" in his belief a short four years later to support same-sex weddings. Neither of those positions was considered bigoted at the time, but the original one is, now. Hillary Clinton experienced the same metamorphosis. (See **Hypocrite**.)

Brendan Eich took the helm of Mozilla only to have the intolerant crowd discover he donated $1,000 to support traditional marriage in 2008. Nobody asked his position now, but in the firestorm that raged after his exposure as a "bigot," he lost his job.

These days, the *bigot* mantra is chanted by intolerant, hypocritical leftists while they destroy statues and deface monuments of those they claim to fight for, like the 54th Regiment Memorial in Boston. Point one finger at me and you have three pointing back at you.

He that cannot reason is a fool. He that will not is a bigot. He that dare not is a slave.

—Andrew Carnegie

Bill

Noun

A bill is a draft of proposed legislation to be approved (or voted down) in committee or, eventually, in the legislative body and signed by the governor of the state or the president of the country into law.

Key words to keep in mind: "draft" and "approval." A draft is not final. Its purpose is to lay the groundwork of an idea that will be added to or subtracted from. Only after studying the content of the final draft should approval ever be given.

The Speaker of the House, Nancy Pelosi, disagrees, saying about the 2,700-page Obamacare bill:

> But we have to pass the bill so you can find out what is in it, away from the fog of the controversy.

Not only does Pelosi need a lesson in the definition of "bill" but also in the definition of "controversy," which is not a fog but in this usage exploration, comprehension, and suggestion, that is, the exercise of reason. Imagine if we applied Pelosi's logic to other aspects of life:

- I have to run a marathon to find out if I need to train for a marathon.
- I have to marry the man so I can find out if I even like the man.
- I must taste the substance in the bottle labeled "arsenic" before I can find out what the label states.

The purpose of a presenting a bill to a legislative body is precisely for criticism, debate, and correction. At the very least, one should read it. Otherwise, they would simply be writing laws—something those in power would most likely much prefer to do!

Bill of Rights

Political term

The Bill of Rights is the first 10 amendments to the U.S. Constitution. It codifies express rights of the people and limits the power of the U.S. government.

The Bill of Rights was a hotly contested issue during the Constitutional Convention. James Monroe insisted on it as a preservation of citizens' autonomy, while others argued the amendments were unnecessary. In the end, Monroe stood his ground, and the Bill of Rights was ratified effective on December 15, 1791. Now Americans' rights are challenged at all levels, and we rely on our Bill of Rights, particularly when arguing issues like gun control (#2) and privacy (#4).

> *A Bill of Rights is what the people are entitled to against every government, and what no just government should refuse, or rest on inference.*
>
> —Thomas Jefferson

#BillOfRights, #Constitution

Bipartisan

Adjective

Traditionally the word for agreement found between opposing views, particularly in politics, bipartisan has come more recently to mean caving of conservative ideology.

Bipartisanship is a sweet notion that can make you feel all warm and tingly, like blood from a fresh cut. Politicians toss it out in an attempt to show a can-do attitude, but it has come to represent capitulation and cowardice. The Gang of Eight immigration reform bill was *bipartisan.*

> *In any compromise between good and evil, it is only evil that can profit.*
>
> —Ayn Rand

President Obama campaigned on the con of bipartisanship with his endless statements of "reaching across the aisle" and "there's not a red America or a blue America, there's just the United States of America." However, once elected, he proceeded to divide the country even more, ramming through Obamacare without a single Republican vote.

His partner in this crime, Harry Reid, used his position as Senate majority leader to keep over 300 bills passed in the House (with bipartisan support) from going to the Senate floor for a vote.

> *It's nice to say let's be bipartisan. But we're a partisan nation. We were raised as a partisan nation.*
>
> —Colin Powell

Black Lives MAGA

Noun

A new term coined by lawyer and civil rights activist Rogan O'Handley (@DC Draino) intended to combat the negativity generated by the phrase "Black Lives Matter." When insisting that Black Lives Matter, especially to the exclusion that all lives matter, the inference is that without white champions, black people are incapable and weak. To combat this narrative, BLMAGA, EBLM (Every Black Life Matters/EveryBLM.com), and other organizations have sprung up to celebrate and support conservative values of life and character rather than melanin content.

> *The idea that BLM would call the greatest genocide of African Americans any sort of Justice, should concern any person of conscience, regardless of color.*
>
> —Neil Mammen, founder, EBLM

Black Lives Matter (BLM)

Global political organization

Black Lives Matter was born in 2013 out of the leftists' insistence that America is systemically racist. Enraged by the deaths of black individuals Treyvon Martin and Michael Brown, the movement found resonance in the mainstream media. It calls for nonviolence, even while inciting it. Without offering a better "system," BLM advocates for the destruction of Western civilization, starting with tearing down statues of famous southerners or well-known slave-owners but never stopping there. They tore down the statues of Civil War hero General U. S. Grant and Frederick Douglas, a black man who fought hard against slavery and for the empowerment of black individuals. Several protests organized by this group ended with rioting and looting. They are communist at root, which positions them as antithetical to America. Their website describes them as "comrades" who focus solely on anti-black racism and power. Their motto is singly racist, and if you try to counter that *all* lives matter, you are deemed racist for saying so. (See **Racist**.) But black babies' lives don't matter to them. (Blacks are 13 percent of the general population, while 36 percent of abortions are black babies.) (See **Planned Parenthood**.) And they aren't protesting Chicago's black-on-black violence, but they are lobbying to defund the police, a tactic that worked to give Germany the SS. We must conclude that the only thing that really *matters* to them is power.

Many black individuals have renounced or disclaimed BLM as racist and as having embraced Marxism but not representing blacks. Candace Owens notably criticized BLM for holding up a known criminal as representative of black America.

> *We are unapologetically Black in our positioning. . . . We've committed to struggling together and to imagining and creating a world free of anti-Blackness. . . . We disrupt the Western-prescribed nuclear family structure requirement by supporting each other as extended families and "villages" that collectively care for one another. . . . We foster a queer-affirming network.*
> —BLM Website Statement of Faith

Bleeding heart

Political term

Usually in reference to a liberal, someone who "bleeds" with compassion for the downtrodden.

Blood-letting as a medical practice was discontinued in the late 1800s. Rarely is bleeding ever beneficial. Liberals still try to employ it in civil society, through taxes and regulations. It will never cure society's ills, just like it never really cured any other disease.

The liberal's bleeding heart claims compassion by labeling people as oppressed victims, inculcating them with the idea that they are hopeless without government intervention and inoculating them against effort. This is the opposite of compassionate. They ought to be called back-stabbing, instead of bleeding heart, liberals.

How do we know? The liberal never goes back to evaluate the fruits of their bloodletting. When confronted with truth, they claim it wasn't enough blood, as in the 2016 run for the presidency. The Democrats claim our society has low employment, the middle class is getting squeezed, and the economy's a mess, without touching on the fact their own party has been in charge, through executive fiat, I might add, for eight long years!

Government has spent trillions of dollars on the War on Poverty, and yet, more people are in poverty now than when the "war" began.

It is naive to believe that handing out trillions of dollars is a sustainable endeavor, but logic matters not to bleeding hearts, focused on their "compassionate" feelings of the here-and-now. They do not consider the possible character destruction and massive debt that these programs incur. They do not ask the question, "what happens next?" or "where does the buck stop?"

Personal compassion for the unfortunate is virtuous, but when paid for by others, at gunpoint, in the form of taxes, it simply becomes *theft*. It should also be mentioned that government is the very *least efficient* way of helping the poor that exists.

Encouraging and supporting personal responsibility, ambition, integrity, and ingenuity are the greatest, most efficient ways to help those less fortunate.

Pay mind to your own life, your own health, and wholeness. A bleeding heart is of no help to anyone if it bleeds to death.

—Frederick Buechner

Bolshevik

Noun

Derived from the Russian word meaning "great" in size or scope, *Bolshevik* became the name of the Lenin-led radical left-wing majority group that brought about the Bolshevik Revolution against the bourgeois class and eventually became the Communist Party. They incited the "have-nots" against the "haves" so that eventually no one had anything at all.

You must understand, the leading Bolsheviks who took over Russia were not Russians. They hated Russians. They hated Christians. Driven by ethnic hatred they tortured and slaughtered millions of Russians without a shred of human remorse. It cannot be overstated. Bolshevism committed the greatest human slaughter of all time. The fact that most of the world is ignorant and uncaring about this enormous crime is proof that the global media is in the hands of the perpetrators.

—Aleksandr Solzhenitsyn

Bourgeoisie

Noun

A term meaning the middle or upper-middle class, or property-owners. Marxists hold that the bourgeoisie are in opposition to the poorer working class, or the proletariat, but it takes two to tango: workers needs employers as much as employers need workers. Marx successfully hijacked the term to mean anyone with means—owners of the *means of production*—and incited folks to rebel and seize the factories. But the workers owning the manufacturing is fraught with the challenge of burdensome bureaucracy, which devolves into rule by committee, and we've already seen that play out in communist Soviet Russia, where everything was in short supply and waiting lines formed for anything of value, including food.

Mollie, the white mare, represents the bourgeoisie in George Orwell's *Animal Farm*.

They pretend to pay us, and we pretend to work.

—Old Soviet communist saying

Brexit

Noun

A combination of "Britain" and "Exiting the European Union," Brexit is the nickname for the movement to withdraw England from the greedy clutches of the socialist bureaucrats who seek to control how the French make wine, dictate how the Swiss make chocolate, regulate how the Austrians craft wiener schnitzel, and govern the exact curvature of a banana. Led strongly by Nigel Farage, Boris Johnson later picked up the standard and brought home the election, after the referendum was rejected by not one but two of Britain's prime ministers, who both resigned rather than betray their socialist tendencies. Don't let her party name "conservative" fool you; Theresa May is no conservative by any American standard.

Bully pulpit

Political term

A position of power from which to exert influence. Originally coined by Theodore Roosevelt, "bully" was then slang for "excellent," and the phrase defined the presidency's bully pulpit as a superb platform from which to advocate an agenda.

Known as the Great Communicator, Ronald Reagan was the master at using the bully pulpit to remind us of We the People.

> The greatness of America doesn't begin in Washington; it begins with each of you—in the mighty spirit of free people under God, in the bedrock values you live by each day in your families, neighborhoods, and workplaces. Each of you is an individual worthy of respect, unique and important to the success of America. And only by trusting you, giving you opportunities to climb high and reach for the stars, can we preserve the golden dream of America as the champion of peace and freedom among the nations of the world.

In stark contrast, Barack Obama has used his position at the bully pulpit to actually *bully*:

> ... So if somebody wants to build a coal-powered plant, they can; it's just that it will bankrupt them, because they're going to be charged a huge sum for all that greenhouse gas that's being emitted.

Bullying is bad, but liberals will always excuse bad behavior if it adheres to their agenda. (See **Hypocrite**.)

Cabinet

Noun

A body of advisers for the president, comprising the heads of all executive departments. They are nominated by the president and must be confirmed by a simple majority in the Senate. The current cabinet includes the vice president and the following department heads:

- Attorney general
- Secretary of agriculture
- Secretary of the commerce
- Secretary of defense
- Secretary of education
- Secretary of energy
- Secretary of interior
- Secretary of labor
- Secretary of health and human services
- Secretary of homeland security
- Secretary of housing and urban development
- Secretary of state
- Secretary of transportation
- Secretary of treasury
- Secretary of veterans affairs

There is no explicit mandate in the Constitution for the cabinet; however, Article II gives the president authority to seek outside counsel in which he, "may require the Opinion, in writing, of the principal Officer in each of the executive Departments, upon any subject relating to the Duties of their respective Offices."

George Washington appointed only four people to his cabinet: secretaries of state, treasury, and war and an attorney general. In 164 years—from 1788 to 1952—eight departments were created. From 1953 to 2002 an additional seven were added.

The secretaries wield enormous power that they are free to abuse or neglect. With recent scandals involving the IRS (under the department of treasury), department of veterans affairs, and department of justice, it's clear that *accountability* has left the building. Punishments and firings for transgression and misdeeds are extremely rare, even despite obvious corruption.

Campaign

Noun

An organization working for the purpose of electing a politician or effectuating some societal change, though candidates often allow their campaigns to devolve into orchestrated hit jobs on the opposition, sometimes known as *mudslinging*.

Demonizing for the sake of bumper-sticker slogans ("Bush lied, people died") is disingenuous and feeds only the simple-minded mob. However, quoting candidates' actual statements, "We came; we saw; he died!" (Hillary Clinton about the overthrow of Gaddafi) ought to be encouraged.

Behavior and actions of the campaigns reflect the values and integrity (or lack thereof) of the candidate.

Canceled

Adjective

One of the newest additions in the nasty lexicon of the Left, refers to someone's status after being publicly rejected or dismissed, typically after a misstatement. For instance, Kanye West, a darling of the Left, was recently canceled after indicating his support for Trump. The joke's on them, though—you can't really cancel Kanye. Megyn

Kelly was canceled and removed from the air after commenting on-air, "What is racist? You do get in trouble if you are a white person who puts on blackface for Halloween or a black person who puts on whiteface for Halloween." For this, they canceled her career. But she was targeted, thinking she could play on their side of the aisle after becoming a Fox News star. It was only a matter of time before they shut her up. Governor Northam of Virginia appeared in his yearbook photo in blackface (or a KKK costume—he's never clarified which) and said on-air that he supported killing babies, and no recriminations, proving that the cancel culture is a leftist weapon to silence people.

Canceling someone is a passive-aggressive way of breaking up with someone.

Never apologize to a mob.

—Jordan Peterson

Capitalism

Noun

An economic and political system fueled by competition, where private parties maintain ownership, instead of the state, which allows and fosters freedom, opportunity, growth, and progress in a society.

Capitalism is always evaluated against dreams. Utopia is a dream. It doesn't exist.

—Rush Limbaugh

Critics depict capitalism as ruthless and heartless because with it comes winners and losers, and in the minds of statists, nobody should ever lose. The statist's utopian dream believes everyone is equal in every single way under the sun, with a unicorn in every backyard and rainbow juice in every refrigerator. In a free-market capitalist society, only a small percentage may have rainbow juice, but it is because of that small percentage that a great many more people have refrigerators.

The statist wishes to eradicate greed; the capitalist understands the futility of this and recommends harnessing that incredible power, coupled with the freedom to pursue it, for the good of everyone. It's no accident that the business behemoths that have created great wealth originated in the free market of the United States. Capitalism offers *incentive* by rewarding hard work, risk, ambition, intelligence, and creativity. Reward drives entrepreneurs to create. Thus we have Microsoft and Apple, Google and Firefox.

Great examples of the superiority of the capitalist system to any kind of statism (communism, socialism, marxism, etc.) abound. West Germany was far better off economically and socially than East Germany, which was run by the communist Soviet Union. The same applies to North versus South Korea. In fact, much of the former communist world has seen a dramatic increase in productivity and standard of living since abandoning government planning and adopting private ownership. India and China have also experienced sustained growth as a result of implementing capitalistic principles.

> *Capitalism has worked very well. Anyone who wants to move to North Korea is welcome.*
>
> —Bill Gates

Caucus

Noun

A group within a legislative body that seeks to represent a certain interest, candidate, or policy.

During presidential campaigning season, we hear much about the Iowa caucuses. Why? Because it's the first state (beginning in 1972) to choose party nominees.

The caucuses represent only a small portion—usually fewer than one-fifth—of the actual voting population. There is no absentee voting. Caucus voters meet in school gyms, churches, or other public places and cast their votes. Republicans write their choices on slips of paper, while Democrats physically move to different parts of the room designated for a particular candidate.

Despite the hullabaloo surrounding the Iowa caucuses, they are not always accurate predictors of the future nominees. Ronald Reagan lost in 1980, George H. W. Bush came in third in 1988, and John McCain finished fourth in 2008.

The most recent Iowa Democratic caucuses included coin tosses to determine winners. Since when is a coin toss democratic? It's not the Super Bowl after all!

A congressional caucus (officially called congressional member organization [CMO]) advocates for and affects public policy. In the 113th Congress there are 336 caucuses and hundreds more informal member groups. There are racial or ethnic caucuses:

- Congressional Black Caucus
- Congressional Hispanic Caucus
- Congressional Asian Pacific American Caucus

Ideological caucuses:

- Blue Dog Coalition (conservative Democrats)
- New Democrat Coalition (moderate Democrats)
- Congressional Progressive (liberal/leftist Democrats)
- Republican Study Committee (conservative Republicans)
- Republican Main Street Partnership (moderate Republicans)
- Liberty Caucus (libertarian Republicans)

Special interest caucuses, of which there are many, many, many. Here are a few:

- Cranberry Caucus

- Animal Protection Caucus
- Kidney Caucus
- Peanut Caucus

The explosion of the number of congressional caucuses is indicative of the expanse of government and the view that it should put its fingers in every element of society. It's the job of our representatives to address macro issues like immigration and national security, not to meddle and peddle cycling, bourbon, and shellfish. Yes, there are caucuses for those.

What's next? A caucus to propose new caucuses?

CHAZ or CHOP

Noun

The Capitol Hill Autonomous Zone (CHAZ), sometimes known as the Capitol Hill Organized Protest (CHOP), was an area in Seattle near its statehouse that was taken over by a rogue element of activists who banished the police, citing their hatred for authority. They promptly established their own militarized enforcement gang, armed with Uzis and AK-47s, because they hypocritically love their own authority. The Democratic mayor of Seattle chose to side with the activists, claiming CHAZ was just like any block party. I've never been to a block party where people died, stores were looted, or riots occurred, have you?

The funniest part of the CHAZ was the ridiculous garden that the misfits planted. Proving the lie that billionaire activist Michael Bloomberg famously sermonized—that farming is so easy, all you do is dig a hole and throw some seeds in—the CHAZ communists tried and failed, miserably, and pretty soon after were begging for food.

Don't forget about the innocent locals whose neighborhoods became caught in the struggle, because they never asked for their Starbucks to burn down.

Checks and balances

Political jargon

A process designed to ensure balance within a political system, whereby power is kept out of the hands of one specific person or group.

Our Founding Fathers knew the danger of power concentrated in the hands of one man and specifically designed the American political system to avoid it. The Constitution divides the government into three branches: legislative, executive, and judicial. Distinct in their roles, but not independent, each must answer for its actions to the other branches.

However, as the executive grows (see **Executive branch**) in the number and size of departments and agencies, it becomes increasingly difficult to check and restrain its actions.

Our carefully constructed system of checks and balances is being negated by the rise of a fourth branch, an administrative state of sprawling departments and agencies that govern with increasing autonomy and decreasing transparency.

—Jonathan Turley, Harvard constitutional law scholar

Christianity

Religion; noun

The religion based on following Jesus Christ, the son of God and a sinless man, who was crucified as punishment for the sins of mankind and resurrected from the dead. It is through the example of His death and resurrection that man can experience grace, mercy, forgiveness, and reconciliation with God. Jesus taught that man must love God and love his neighbor. Christianity is based on the Bible, which is the most reliable history text in the world and has never been disproven, though many have tried.

Because the Christian message is focused on selflessness, many secularists and atheists, through their reckless, self-righteous pride, condemn Christianity because it so strongly opposes their humanist worldview. Humanists propose that each person is his own god, which, of course, is extremely dangerous, especially when those types of folks amass power.

> *As long as you are proud you cannot know God. A proud man is always looking down on thing and people: and, of course, as long as you are looking down you cannot see something that is above you.*
>
> —C. S. Lewis, *Mere Christianity*

#Apologetics, #ReasonableFaith, #Morality

Cisgender/Cissexual/Cis

Adjective

A person whose gender corresponds to his/her genitalia, the sex they were "assigned," or observed to have, at birth. The opposite of *transgender*, the word is a veiled implication that "normal" is weird.

Climate change

Noun

An alarmist effort to control the population through fear-mongering and falsified data. How do we know this? Because it was called global cooling, then global warming, then *climate change*. It presupposes two things: (1) the Earth is warming—for this there is no reliable data, (2) warming or change in climate is anthropogenic, or human caused—for this there is no proof. A third factor is the assumption that the temperature of the Earth is perfect right now. But I'm sure many Brits would like to return to the warmer day of growing their own grapes. For me, I'm personally always a little cold, so I only wish it could be true. (See **Global warming**.)

College

Noun

An institution of higher learning, after high school, where students focus on a specific field of study to gain a bachelor's degree.

A bachelor's degree in the fields of biology, chemistry, physics, or electrical engineering demonstrates a level of higher learning. Advanced study is typically necessary in these technical fields to gain the required knowledge to pursue a related career in the real world, though it is becoming more and more apparent that learning can happen outside the university. Unfortunately, there is a slew of majors that are relevant only in the bubble of university life: women's studies, gender studies, and cultural studies—pick a culture, any culture—except American, of course.

Any class within the departments of cultural or women's something-or-other is most surely a class you might confuse with a *Saturday Night Live* skit. It's shocking that people all across the country are spending tens of thousands of dollars to learn about and discuss a topic they could plunk down ten dollars for at a comedy club:

- GaGa for Gaga: Sex, Gender, and Identity (University of Virginia)
- Invented Languages: Klingon and Beyond (University of Texas)
- Politicizing Beyonce (Rutgers)
- Getting Dressed (Princeton) If students at an Ivy League college haven't yet figured out how to get dressed, it's time we questioned Princeton's entrance requirements.

Once upon a time, colleges were places to learn how to think critically, debate your viewpoint, and evaluate alternative positions. They were places of intellectual stimulation and growth. In a majority of American colleges and universities, that is no longer the case. (There are a few certain exceptions, which we won't discuss here.)

No longer are all points of view welcome. Rather, any point of view that deviates from the leftist politically correct agenda is silenced. Many schools have enacted speech codes that limit or ban verbal or written expression of opposing views on race, gender, sex, immigration, religion, the military, the economy, the environment, fraternities, gaming, exercise, food, children, and even "inappropriately directed laughter." Basically, anything the statists (because a university is in many regards an example of a utopian state) find insulting, offensive, or annoying.

Fear not, they've also created "free speech zones," a tiny area on campus, like a hopscotch square, where one is free to express one's views—as long as it's not too offensive to somebody, somewhere. "Trigger warnings" are now all the rage, informing students of potentially offensive words (like "man" to a feminist). There are also "safe places" (in case they miss the trigger warning) to protect them—not from the sticks and stones that may break their bones—but from words that hurt a 20-year-old's feelings. Microaggression is the new dog whistle for progressives, who have advanced so far that they can perceive insult even when no one else can. This has the unintended result of producing simpering, sniveling babies who are convinced they are always right, incapable of growth or maturity.

The ideological bias and hostility toward dissenters are evidenced by a number of invited speakers who were boycotted. Ayaan Hirsi Ali, an outspoken critic of Islam's treatment of women and crusader for women's rights, was invited to give the commencement speech at Brandeis University in May 2014. After a moblike campaign of vilification and threats of violence, the university president withdrew the invitation.

In that same year, Rutgers invited former Secretary of State and National Security Adviser Condoleeza Rice to receive an honorary degree. In a rousing display of leftist "tolerance," the students threw a tantrum saying Rice was complicit in war crimes. Rice gracefully withdrew as she did not want to cause an uproar during their commencement period.

Universities, the progressives' promised land, the compassionate open-minded souls fighting for the ignored and oppressed, the champions of women and minorities threw a hissy fit and silenced two black women. Have they banned the word "hypocrisy" in their speech codes? Do they no longer teach irony in their literary classes?

> *My mother said I must always be intolerant of ignorance but understanding of illiteracy. That some people, unable to go to school, were more educated and more intelligent than college professors.*
>
> —Maya Angelou

Cohorts

Noun

A term used for the newly created groups of kids that were allowed to return to schools (mostly private) under the newly designed "hybrid" models put forth by the geniuses on schools' boards of directors. The hybrid models differ from school to school, depending largely on the intelligence and preferences of said geniuses. Some cohorts attended in person two days a week or one week in person and two weeks virtual. At the publication of this book, there are still more hybrid versions being developed by "really smart" people who have no experience in these matters.

Common Core

Noun

The biggest overhaul of our education system in history. Costing billions of dollars, implemented without any testing of its efficacy, Common Core uses new methods for teaching time-worn truths, at the very cost of said truths. In short, it promised everything and delivered worse than nothing, as test scores are now lower than before. But hey, if they just change the standards, everybody gets a trophy!

It's no wonder the United States is 27th in world academics rankings.

Michael Mulgrew, president of the United Federation of Teachers, speaking at their convention (about parents' skepticism of Common Core), said: "I'm gonna punch you in the face and push you in the dirt because this is the teachers! These are our tools!"

When teachers become the bullies, everyone wins.

Catchphrase: "Because, who *doesn't* want their child to be common?"

#CommonCore, #Education, #Bullying

Congress

Noun

Comprised of the Senate and House of Representatives, Congress is the bicameral legislative body of the U.S. government with its responsibilities and duties outlined in Article I of the Constitution. The structure of a *bicameral* (two-sided) body was agreed to at the Constitutional Convention of 1787 in what is known as the Great Compromise.

The question was: How many representatives should each state have? The Virginia Plan called for a varying number based on population of the state. The New Jersey Plan suggested a fixed number from each. Needless to say, the more populous states favored the Virginia Plan, while the less populous states supported the New Jersey Plan. Enter the compromise: Each state would send two representatives to the Senate and a proportional representation to the House.

The House of Representatives was designed specifically to be "of the people" because representatives were directly elected (the Senate, until 1913, was elected by state legislatures). In contrast to a six-year term a senator serves, a member of the House serves only two. This was to allow for a more accurate representation of the people as public opinion turns.

Although term limits are not addressed in the Constitution, they were in its precursor, the Articles of Confederation. It stated: "No person shall be capable of being a delegate for more than three years in any term of six years." The drafters would've done well to keep that principle in place.

Serving the nation as a public servant is honorable and noble; however, it can, and has, become a lifelong career endeavor for many, which has resulted in a ruling class of elites who sometime think they are above the law. There are House and Senate members who have held their office for decades—some still in office at the time of this writing:

- Senator John McCain—29 years
- Representative Barney Frank—32 years
- Representative Ralph Hall—34 years (defeated at age 91)
- Representative Charles Rangel—44 years
- Senator Patrick Leahy—39 years
- Senator Thad Cochran—37 years
- Senator Robert Byrd—51 years (the longest in Senate history)
- Representative John Dingell—53 years (the longest in House history)

The longer one stays in office, the more clout they hold. The more clout they hold, the more likely lobbyists and big donors will throw money their way to keep them in power. The longer they're in power, the more they'll do to stay in power. A quest for power leads to maneuvering for positions on powerful committees, quid pro quos with donors, attempts at redistricting, and various other corrupting influences. The focus shifts from how best to serve the people to how best to serve themselves. It's a vicious cycle.

The human flaws of selfishness and greed are ever present. To ignore them is to foster them. The delegates at the Constitutional Convention did not heed the warning of Thomas Jefferson when he wrote, "I dislike, and strongly dislike . . . the abandonment, in every instance, of the principle of rotation in office, and most particularly in the case of the President."

We've limited the president; it's time to do the same for Congress.

Suppose you were an idiot, and suppose you were a member of Congress; but I repeat myself.

—Mark Twain

#TermLimits

Conservatism

Adjective

A philosophical view that embraces the ideals of small government and individual freedom, coupled with personal responsibility. It is not a party line. It is the bedrock of American values: life, liberty, and the pursuit of happiness, as rights granted by our Creator, *not* the government.

Conservatism starts with the principle of seeing the world as it is, not as something we dream of. It is about betterment, not perfection. Perfection is unachievable. Conservatism focuses on encouraging individuals to better themselves, thereby improving society.

Conservatives seek to conserve the founding principles of the nation, always aware that if it were the government that granted our rights, it can also take them away. Lately conservatism has been somewhat perverted. For the purposes of this book, conservatism means preservation of freedom, or *freedomism.* Freedom is the ultimate bedrock for prosperity and happiness.

Conservatives do not look to government and politics for meaning. They look to their own lives—their families, their work, their friends, their hobbies, and most of all, their God-based religions.

—Dennis Prager

Convention

Noun

A meeting or assembly of delegates, often referring to presidential candidate nominations.

By the time the convention rolls around, the nominee usually has clearly emerged, but the delegates' vote makes it official. At the convention, the party's platform is announced and adopted, and the rules and procedures for the next election cycle are determined.

That's fun stuff for political wonks, but for the bulk of America, a presidential convention kick-starts their interest in the general election. Balloons fly, music roars, and great speechifying takes place. Or, in Barack Obama's case, a royal coronation set against the backdrop of imperial Greek columns. Nothing scary or totalitarian there.

With party up-and-comers and Hollywood celebrities rounding out the roster, the convention rallies the base and, except in the notable 2012 Democratic case, celebrates the process of our great republic.

Here's the story: At the 2012 Democratic convention, the party adopted a platform that left out the word "God" and did not mention Jerusalem as the capital of Israel. They then decided this would be an indefensible position in the election cycle and determined to reinstate God and Jerusalem. The Los Angeles mayor led a voice vote from the large stage. After the motion was vociferously voted down thrice, he forcefully declared victory and reinstated God in the platform. So much for democracy! The video is quite entertaining: https://www.youtube.com/watch?v=t8BwqzzqcDs.

Constitution

Noun

The document that provides the practical application of the principles of our government. The promises of life, liberty, and the pursuit of happiness, referenced in the Declaration of Independence, are fulfilled in the Constitution. It does not *grant* our rights; it *protects* them, stating: "We the people of the United States, in order to form a more perfect union, . . . *secure* the blessings of liberty to ourselves and our posterity."

Written in 1787 and officially ratified in 1788, the Constitution consists of seven articles that address the duties, responsibilities, and *limits* of government.

Article I—The legislative branch, that is, Congress. Established the bicameral body of the House of Representatives and Senate and their respective requirements, duties, and restrictions and processes for bill origination and passage.

Article II—The executive branch. Established the requirements, duties, restrictions, and electoral process of the president.

Article III—The judicial branch. Established the Supreme Court and federal courts.

Article IV—Addressed the obligations of states, the addition of new states, and the federal government's authority in relation to them.

Article V—Established the authorization for Congress or a convention of state legislatures to propose amendments to the Constitution.

Article VI—Established the supremacy of federal laws.

Article VII—Explained how many states were needed (nine) to ratify and put the Constitution into effect.

Some believe the Constitution is malleable, "a living document," and may be interpreted through the lens of society's changing views. That is an ignorant and dangerous position. The bedrock of a government cannot change because a certain president wants more power, or a certain party wants to pass legislation, or a judge wants to make law from the bench. That's a wrecking ball on the foundation of your house.

The Framers were no fools; they foresaw the potential for power grabs, so they included Article V, which allows for structured change instead of haphazard, fickle changes.

The Constitution is a solid framework that has sustained the most successful, freest nation for more than 200 years. It is not to be tampered with.

Our Constitution was made only for a moral and religious people. It is wholly inadequate to the government of any other.
—John Adams to Massachusetts Militia, October 11, 1798

Coronavirus

Noun

The newest strain of a highly infectious type of virus that originated in Wuhan, China. Alternately known as the "Chinese Flu," "Kung Flu," "Wuhan Coronavirus," "Shanghai Shingles," and COVID-19.

This virus is reportedly much more contagious and deadly than previous versions. Reacting to wild predictions of millions of deaths, governments the world over sought to shut down (as much as possible) all human interaction, consequently paralyzing entire nations' economies.

Dr. Ezekiel Emanuel, Obamacare architect, said: "Realistically, COVID-19 will be here for the next 18 months or more. We will not be able to return to normalcy until we find a vaccine or effective medications. . . . Is all that economic pain worth trying to stop COVID-19? The truth is we have no choice."

Typically, in the United States, we pride ourselves on having choices, but we allowed the government to box us in without even a raised hand to question. Some say the mainstream media (MSM) was complicit, influenced by Chinese financing. They asked questions like, "Why do you call it the Chinese virus," to which Trump answered, "Because it comes from China." He elaborated that the

Chinese were running a misdirection campaign to point figures at the U.S. military, and he wouldn't allow that.

In some U.S. areas, governments mandated citizen behavior, enforced "stay-at-home" restrictions, and ticketed and arrested people worshipping, even in their cars. New Jersey Governor Phil Murphy, on his rationale for the coronavirus lockdown, said, "*I wasn't thinking of the Bill of Rights* when we did this." Uhm, there's a Constitution that prohibits megalomaniacal, tyrannical actions like these.

In many states, abortion services were deemed "essential," while other surgeries were "nonessential." The Michigan governor defended this position, calling abortion "life sustaining."

The privilege to dictate which people are "allowed" to work and which are not is not delineated in the Constitution; therefore, the government does not have it. But a docile, well-schooled, and fearful public obeys. Citizens really should read the Constitution more and listen to the MSM less.

> *If people don't think they have the power to solve their problems, they won't even think about how to solve them.*
>
> —Saul D. Alinsky

#Coronavirus, #COVID19, #ChinaFlu, #WuhanFlu, #CCP_is_terrorist, #ChineseCommunistParty

Covidiot

Noun

A term coined by nationally syndicated radio host Chris Plante to mean people so consumed by fear that they refuse to look at scientific evidence and blindly follow the recommendations of a select group of elites who feed their fears, thus rendering them idiotic—incapable of reason. (See also **Karen.**)

Creepy porn lawyer (CPL)

Noun

Tucker Carlson's term for Michael Avenatti, who was Stormy Daniels' lawyer for her suit against Donald Trump, in which she alleged that he raped her. The ruling had her paying Trump—maybe the first time a porn star paid for sex—but although Avenatti lost, he became a left wing darling, appearing on CNN a zillion times. And then he went to jail, because justice prevailed.

Critical race theory (CRT)

Noun

The theory that for white people, there is no escaping racism, and their guilt and bloody hands disqualify them from holding any positions of power (unless they are approved of by a governing [read Marxist] body). CRT blames crime on the system, that if there were no laws, there would be no lawbreakers. Of course, this is true, but it kind of defeats the purpose: to uphold right and wrong. That's why we've seen so many CRT supporters also in strong favor of defunding the police. To hold someone accountable for misdeeds is not racist, it's just common sense, something the Left struggles with.

> *Students in our universities are inundated with Critical Race Theory. This is a Marxist doctrine, holding that America is a wicked and racist nation, that even young children are complicit in oppression, and that our entire society must be radically transformed. . . . A perfect example of critical race theory was recently published by the Smithsonian Institution. This document alleged that concepts such as hard work, rational thinking, and the nuclear family and belief in God were not values that unite all Americans, but were instead aspects of "whiteness."*
>
> —President Donald J. Trump

Cronyism/Crony capitalism

Noun

Special privileges, rewards, appointments, or authority awarded based on favors and friendship not merit or qualifications.

Cronyism continues to grow with the expanse of government. A large government with broad taxation and regulation powers has people clamoring for favors, exemptions, and a reprieve from the forceful hammer (and sickle?) of the government. Politicians on both sides of the aisle make promises of subsidies, preferential tax treatment, and relaxed regulations in return for political support.

The result is wasted money on unproductive endeavors and a disintegration of public trust. Crony capitalism is cronyism as applied to big business, when businesses curry favor from big government. It is also an attempt to smear the word "capitalism," similar to social "justice" or political "correctness," as if those words demand modifiers. Clearly, though, these are *not* capitalist, *not* justice, and *incorrect*. Oh, and we can add "microaggression" to the list, now, too! For example:

- At a rally of Hispanic voters in 2010, President Obama said, "We're going to punish our enemies and reward our friends who stand with us on issues that are important to us."
- In his push for advancing renewable energy companies and "green jobs," $16.4 billion of the $20.5 billion in loans from the Department of Energy Loans went to companies owned or run by Obama backers, after he *promised* to "bankrupt" coal companies. The General Accountability Office (GAO) determined that the DOE "had treated applicants inconsistently in the application review process, favoring some applicants and disadvantaging others." And the inspector general testified that contracts have been steered to "friends and family."

#Cronyism, #EthicsMatter

Crusades

Noun

Holy wars fought from 1095 to 1272, also known as the worst example of Christian behavior that Obama could find in order to laud Islam as the "peaceful" religion.

Former Dixie Professor of Ecclesiastical History at Cambridge and the most respected scholar on the subject of the Crusades, Jonathan Riley-Smith, *defines them* as "[w]ar-pilgrimages proclaimed by the Popes on Christ's behalf and waged for the recovery of Christian territory or people, or in their defense."

Recovery and *defense.* The Crusades were the Church's answer to the conquering, pillaging, enslavement, and torture that invading Muslim armies visited on Christian settlements over hundreds of years. By the end of the eleventh century, Muslims had taken all of Christian North Africa, the Middle East, Asia Minor, and most of Spain. They had conquered, by the sword, two-thirds of the (previously) Christian world. Pope Urban II called for the First Crusade in 1095 to stop the carnage. In his speech at the Council of Clermont, he explained that Muslims had

> invaded the lands of those Christians and has depopulated them by the sword, pillage and fire. . . . [I]t has either entirely destroyed the churches of God or appropriated them for the rites of its own religion. . . . When they wish to torture people by a base death, they perforate their navels, and dragging forth the extremity of the intestines, bind it to a stake; then with flogging they lead the victim around until the viscera having gushed forth [and] the victim falls prostrate upon the ground. . . . What shall I say of the abominable rape of the women? To speak of it is worse than to be silent. The kingdom of the Greeks is now dismembered by them and deprived of territory so vast in extent that it can not be traversed in a march of two months.

This is the (often-ignored) explanation for the Crusades. Seeking to deride Christianity, many portray the Crusades as a mission of self-righteous, intolerant imperialism, but if accusations of pillaging and plundering, rape, torture, conquering, and enslavement are staples of Crusade condemnation, then they should start with the invading Muslims.

The Crusades were a *response* to Muslim aggression. Rather than surrender to Islamic conquest and submit to its rule, Christendom defended itself and its followers, who were unjustly targeted for their beliefs.

The Crusades were similar to the Allies' response to Hitler's Germany. We don't label World War II as an aggressive offensive fought to torture, kill, conquer, and convert, because it was a *just* war waged in recovery and defense, like the Crusades.

Cultural literacy

Noun

A term coined by American literary critic E. D. Hirsch, it's the fluency in the common vernacular and customs in a given society. Analogous to simple literacy, cultural literacy is required for participation in and effecting the direction of a nation, which is why you are reading this book!

Dark horse

Noun

A long shot or underdog candidate. The phrase originates from the world of horse racing. Trainers and jockeys would keep a particularly fast horse from public view, training it "in the dark." They then entered it in the race at quite favorable odds, thereby maximizing their payoff.

Dark horse took on political meaning in 1844 with the nomination of James K. Polk. After numerous votes at the Democratic Convention were taken, neither front-runner Martin Van Buren nor Lewis Cass could get the required two-thirds vote, and Polk was suggested as a compromise. The Whig Party mocked him, printing newspapers asking who he was, recklessly giving him intense publicity. In the end, Polk won the presidency.

Deficit

Noun

The shortfall of money between what the government collects in taxes and fines and the amount it spends. The national debt is the accumulation of deficits.

In the past, spending that exceeded revenue primarily financed wars and stopped when the war ended. Not so today. Since 1930, only during the Eisenhower and Clinton presidencies has the government not run a deficit. And since the mid-1960s, the main culprits driving spending are entitlement programs: Social Security, Medicare/Medicaid, and welfare. These are promises made yesterday to take care of people today using borrowed money from tomorrow.

Perhaps they're hoping climate change will somehow produce money-growing trees.

Liberals insist on raising taxes to fund the bloated budget, but they could tax the "one percenters" at 100 percent and still not cover expenditures. The only solution is to cut spending. Cut, slash, take a knife, hatchet, machete, and chainsaw to the overextended, unnecessary, unaccountable, wasteful spending of Washington, because this continuing mismanagement and irresponsibility are unsustainable. Just search the Internet for "wastebook" to read about ridiculous government waste in action.

> *The goal is to reduce the size and scope of government spending, not to focus on the deficit. The deficit is the symptom of the disease.*
>
> —Grover Norquist

Delegate

Noun

An elected or appointed person who represents a country, state, or person.

Delegates to the presidential nominating conventions are often party activists or local political leaders and are chosen in a variety of ways, rules differing in each party and each state.

For most states, the Republican Party employs the winner-take-all system, meaning delegates will cast their votes for the candidate who won their state in the primary or caucus. There are a few exceptions, California being one, where the state allocates delegates proportionally based on the candidates' percentage of votes in the state.

Democrats cast their votes proportionally at the convention.

Demagogue

Noun/verb

From the Greek *demos*, meaning "people/folk," and *ago*, meaning "manipulate," a demagogue is the people's manipulator, and to a demagogue, an issue is to obscure or mutate it such that it serves an ideology.

Demagogues seek power and control by appealing to emotion. They stir up fear, selfishness, and prejudice through lies, accusations, and exploitation. Facts, reason, and civility lie abandoned to their ideological quest for power. President Obama is regularly labeled a demagogue. And for good reason. The best example is his regular recitations to push the Affordable Care Act: "If you like your plan, you can keep your plan. If you like your doctor, you can keep your doctor."

These statements were not mistakes or misunderstandings of the legislation—he knew them to be untrue when he said them. According to one of the policy advisers of Obamacare, Jonathan Gruber, the only way to garner support for Obamacare relied on "the stupidity of the American voter," because, "lack of transparency is a huge political advantage." Gruber exhibited demagoguery brilliantly.

President Obama's most disgraceful display of demagoguery was following the terrorist attack on our consulate in Benghazi, Libya. Four Americans were killed in a planned attack by Islamist terrorists, but the truth did not fit Obama's narrative that the terrorists were on the run, so he blamed an Internet video. He and his administration claimed that the attack was a spontaneous response to a video criticizing Muslims. He lied about the state of the war on terror and the murder of four men. Why?

To win an election. Weeks after it was well known that the video had nothing to do with the planned attack, he continued to tell his fairytale. Why?

Because there were people willing to believe it, and demagoguery tends to be a one-way street. A demagogue (not to be confused with demigod) never apologizes.

Not to be outdone by the demagogue in chief, Secretary of State Hillary Clinton chimed in by assuring the parents of murdered Navy SEAL Tyrone Woods that they would arrest and punish the filmmaker—the filmmaker of a film that she *knew* had absolutely nothing to do with the attack.

In a June 2015 address at Texas Southern University, Hillary Clinton asserted:

> We have a responsibility to say clearly and directly what's really going on in our country . . . a sweeping effort to disempower and disenfranchise people of color, poor people, and young people from one end of our country to another.

She continued with, "Stop fearmongering about a phantom epidemic of election fraud." Fearmongering about voter suppression is acceptable, but showing concern for rampant voter fraud is not! Oh the hypocrisy! Oh the demagoguery!

The more idiots there are in society, the stronger a demagogue becomes. His goal is to evoke a frenzy of fear, anger, and indignation about the condition of society and then present himself as the solution to the "injustice," "unfairness," and "intolerance." The best defenses against a demagogue are knowledge and wisdom.

> *The demagogue is one who preaches doctrines he knows to be untrue to men he knows to be idiots.*
>
> —H. L. Mencken

Democracy

Noun

Mob rule. Democracy has become a catch-all to describe a system of free elections, representative government, and the right to say and do whatever, whenever, and wherever one wants. We often hear, "In a democratic society I have the right to . . . " The term is useful when contrasting a government of elected representatives to tyrannical dictatorships, such as North Korea or Iran. However, in a pure democracy, nobody has the right to anything until it becomes the passion and will of the majority. Democracy is majority rule *without* minority rights. Individuals in the minority have no protection or recourse against the unlimited power of the majority.

Closely tied to his statement about demagoguery, H. L. Mencken wrote:

> The most popular man under a democracy is not the most democratic man, but the most despotic man. The common folk delight in the exactions of such a man. They like him to boss them. Their natural gait is the goosestep.

In essence, a true democracy is a band of bullies ruling a mob fueled by unthinking passion. As a result, democracy can easily lead to tyranny.

The word "democracy" does not appear in the Declaration of Independence or the Constitution because the Framers knew the true meaning and danger of it. The creation of checks and balances, and most important the Bill of Rights, illustrates their aversion to democracy. In Federalist No. 10, James Madison wrote:

> [I]t may be concluded that a pure democracy, by which I mean a society consisting of a small number of citizens, who assemble and administer the government in person, can admit of no cure for the mischiefs of faction. A common passion or interest will, in almost every case, be felt by a majority of the whole; a communication and concert result from the form of government itself; and there is nothing to check the inducements to sacrifice the weaker party or an obnoxious individual. Hence it is that such democracies have ever been spectacles of turbulence and contention: have ever been found incompatible with personal security or the

rights of property; and have in general been as short in their lives as they have been violent in their deaths.

No matter the desires of the majority in the legislature, no matter the whimsical changes of heart of the masses, the God-given rights in those first 10 amendments could not be trampled, changed, or usurped. The Founders of our nation did not intend or fashion democracy but rather a republic. (See **Republic** and **Groupthink**.)

Deplorable

Adjective, noun

Originally an adjective meaning "wretched or contemptable," Hillary Clinton's use of the word in "basket of deplorables" in a 2016 election campaign speech to describe half the supporters of Donald Trump launched it into the mainstream vernacular by prompting many to embrace it as a badge of honor. Eschewing her assessment that they were "racist, sexist, homophobic, xenophobic" and, by inference, stupid, they adopted it as an antilabel, becoming a virtual army of deplorables fighting to elect Trump and putting the lie to the word.

It was what she said after that line that that was more indicative of how the Left views American society. She called them "irredeemable," which implies that those human lives have no value. Indeed, there were many vicious attacks directed against Trump rally attendees. While the Left typically resorts to violence, conservatives seek to ennoble and uplift. In one word, Clinton expressed how the Left views anyone who dissents, but luckily, the public didn't accept the insult. Although Clinton never apologized, insisting, instead, that she regretted saying "half," much to her enduring humiliation, Trump became president and she became, if not completely irrelevant, a sore loser.

Wow, Hillary Clinton was SO INSULTING to my supporters, millions of amazing, hard-working people.

—Trump tweet, September 10, 2016

Ditto/Mega dittos/DittoHead

Noun

A term meaning duplicate, used by Rush Limbaugh and his followers to indicate full agreement. Rush Limbaugh pioneered conservative talk radio, revolutionizing the media and political landscape with his brand of hard-hitting commentary, biting satire, and engaging humor. In an unprecedented and remarkably touching moment in our nation's history, Rush was surprised with the Presidential Medal of Freedom at the State of the Union Speech in 2020, bestowed by First Lady Melania. This made all the liberals' heads explode because they were a captive audience. Trump sure knows how to troll the Democrats.

I won't stop until everyone agrees with me.

—Rush Limbaugh

Drain the swamp

Phrase

Refers to the removal of water from marshy land in the course of development, which consequently clears out all the mosquitoes, alligators, and other swamp dwellers. The metaphor has been adopted by those on all points on the political spectrum who hold that government is full of corruption and deceit and that politicians are similar to pesky insects and swamp creatures. As a political outsider, President Trump made the phrase a lynchpin of his campaign.

We should have to drain the swamp—change the capitalist sys-
tem—if we want to get rid of those mosquitos.

—Victor L. Berger, founding member,

Social Democratic Party of America

Sometimes, when you are up to your elbows in alligators, it
is hard to remember your original objective was to drain the
swamp. I think we can drain the swamp. We can take on the
Washington system. We can change from remote control to per-
sonal control of our lives.

—Ronald Reagan

I will Make Our Government Honest Again—believe me. But
first, I'm going to have to #DrainTheSwamp in DC.

—Donald J. Trump

Dystopia

Noun

The antonym of "utopia": an imagined world where everything is bad, particularly a totalitarian environment under rule by a dictator.

Leftists dream of utopia: perfect material and social equality. Their method of reaching it requires regulation of income, speech, healthcare, education, Internet access, and even lightbulbs. In their utopia, the state deems what is appropriate, acceptable, and true. Liberal utopia *is* dystopia for sane people. Interestingly, state-controlled societies are exactly what wildly popular science fiction novels portray as a dystopia. Many would call *Fahrenheit 451*, *Brave New World*, and *1984* not only entertaining reads but also warnings.

Economy

Noun

The wealth and resources of a country; the production and consumption models in a society.

We often speak of the economy as if it had a mind of its own (which it does): The economy is good, bad. It's in a recession, depression. It's sluggish or recovering. These generalizations are particularly meaningless to the average citizen until they feel it in their pocketbooks as a job loss, price or tax increase, or a drop in real estate value. Eventually, when many people are feeling the bad economy, they look to government to fix it.

The government, however, has a poor history of effectively managing the economy. For instance, the big housing bubble that threatened the U.S. economy in 2008 and onward resulted from, in part, government incentives in the mortgage industry. The government addressed that with such formidable regulations the economy cannot climb out of the doldrums.

Since Franklin Roosevelt's New Deal, the line separating government from the economy has increasingly blurred. Attempts to inject money into, or "stimulate," the economy didn't work then and still don't, not that anyone in government, high on their own *puissance,* would notice. In reality, *shifting* money is the same as redistributing it, which does not *grow* the economy, but strangely, it does grow Wall Street. Wait, weren't they the bad guys?

Government intruding into private enterprise with heavy taxation and burdensome regulations does not increase profits, create jobs, or encourage entrepreneurship; it stifles them all.

There's a saying in the theater, *There are no small parts—only small actors.* Government does not comprehend that statement. It was scripted as a small role in our economy, but the government, lest it be thought small, stole everyone's props, intruded into scenes, seized dialogue, and upstaged and blocked the real stars. Our prima donna government doesn't enhance the show. It ruins it.

The best way for government to help improve the economy is to exit, stage left.

> *Government's view of the economy could be summed up in a few short phrases: If it moves, tax it. If it keeps moving, regulate it. And if it stops moving, subsidize it.*
>
> —Ronald Reagan

Education

Noun

The teaching or informing a person on any subject or concept such that they become capable of instructing someone else. As a concept, education should be pursued, admired, and celebrated, but it is not a cure-all for every problem that plagues society. Calls for more funding, more standards, subsidized college, and mandatory preschool are coupled with outlandish claims that education will annihilate poverty, crime, unemployment, sexism, racism, and terrorism.

False. Many of those problems are rooted in a lack of morality and values. They stem from an individual's behavior and choices, not from a lack of knowledge. For example, the young man knows that stealing is wrong, but he wants what he wants and has limited moral discernment.

Too high a value has been placed on our educational *system*. After several overhauls over decades that resulted in only further failings in students' academic achievement, the bloated education bureaucracy has most recently implemented Common Core, which attempts to homogenize learning by implementing an untested one-size-fits-all curriculum and abandoning traditional, proven methods of teaching. (See **Common Core**.)

Education has erroneously become synonymous with knowledge, definitively demonstrating the pathetic failures of our government system. We don't have education. We have schooling. This results in an inability to process anything that disagrees with a young person's knowledge base, which has given rise to the silencing of speech and "safe spaces" for the easily offended.

Without education we are in a horrible and deadly danger of taking educated people seriously.

—G. K. Chesterton

An education should be a lifelong endeavor of learning, honing skills, and thinking critically. An honest education leads to wisdom.

It is the mark of an educated mind to be able to entertain a thought without accepting it.

—Aristotle

Education is the ability to listen to almost anything without losing your temper or your self-confidence.

—Robert Frost

Electorate

Noun

The body of people entitled to vote in an election. Some resources define the term as "those qualified to vote." In the United States, the qualifications to be part of the electorate are minimal: a citizen 18 years of age and not a felon is qualified to vote. One need not be knowledgeable, informed, or even sane to join the electorate.

The term is often more narrowly used to describe those who are expected to or have voted, which tremendously shrinks the number value of the electorate. But civic health is not specifically linked to high voter turnout.

Get Out the Vote successfully encouraged people to exercise their voting rights (but remarkably, not their thinking ability), and the U.S. electorate chose an inexperienced narcissist in Obama, who precipitated the steady decline of our country's position in the world.

Being a part of the electorate is a right, but it's a right that should be taken more seriously than clicking "Like" on a Facebook post. We need a serious review of our qualifications for voting.

When the people find that they can vote themselves money that will herald the end of the republic.

—Benjamin Franklin

Impress upon children the truth that the exercise of the elective franchise is a social duty of as solemn a nature as man can be called to perform; that a man may not innocently trifle with his vote; that every elector is a trustee as well for others as himself and that every measure he supports has an important bearing on the interests of others as well as on his own.

—Daniel Webster

Emotional support animal

Noun

Any (apparently) animal that anyone claims offers them therapeutic support, typically for elderly or disabled people, but recently expanded to all. Branded by Adam Corolla in his book, *I'm Your Emotional Support Animal: Navigating Our All Woke, No Joke Culture*, the support animal comes in all kinds and provides an illuminating look at the fragility of our species these days. It used to be that folks wouldn't care to admit they needed to pet something to feel calmer. Now it seems like a badge of merit to claim an "emotional/mental need" to have your support rabbit, or lizard, or hedgehog.

No, those aren't jokes. As Corolla's book indicates, no humor is allowed anymore.

Environment (Environmentalist)

Noun

The surroundings in which a person, animal, or thing exists. It is the air, weather, trees, flowers, mountains, and water; it is the world in which we live. It is beautiful, valuable, and worthy of care.

Environmentalists find themselves highly preoccupied with the condition of the environment at the expense of the condition of humanity. To this end, they embrace the theory of imminent, apocalyptic world-ending destruction, currently known as "climate change." (See **Climate change**, **Global cooling**, and **Global warming**.) As their worship and reverence of nature increases, they increasingly view humans as the problem. If you scratch below the surface of an environmentalist zealot, you are likely to find someone in favor of exterminating humanity. Just say, "You first."

They care less about *actual* diseases, like malaria, which has killed millions of people in Africa, and more about limiting human advancement, like wiping out malaria with DDT, as was done effectively in the United States.

The recent Californian man-made drought is a perfect example of lack of regard for the future of mankind (water infrastructure) but overconcern for three-inch, nonindigenous baitfish. Starve the farmers, save the delta smelts.

Environmentalists also ignore the great good that human progress has had on the planet, like saving species from extinction (bald eagles and peregrine falcons now flourish).

There is little doubt that we should be responsible in the stewardship of our planet, but humanity gives the environment meaning. We should stick around to make sure the planet does, too.

Equality

Noun

Having the same value or worth.

Many couple the term "equality" with fairness, claiming that the rich need to pay their "fair share" or it's not fair to gay people when a Christian bakery, florist, or photographer refuses to participate in a gay wedding. However, the leftists' argument for equality is actually an argument *against* fairness.

A person spends years building a business, risking everything, and working long, hard days and then has to pay to fund programs for people unwilling to take a similar risk and put in that same hard work? Is that fair?

Is it *fair* when an employee at the local grocery store goes above and beyond to attain a raise and then the government mandates a *minimum wage* increase giving all the mediocre and subpar coworkers the same pay as the hard worker?

The Left's version of fairness is the antithesis of equality. They champion the underdog, the so-called little guy, and demand *special* treatment for them in schools, the workplace, and courts. They want to take money away from someone who earns it and give it to someone who hasn't earned it.

In essence, the leftist's position is to encourage inequality as a means to achieving equality. Sounds fair.

Gender equality: Men and women are the same, so they should be paid the same. *Therefore, government should pass legislation to guarantee women's wages.*

Men and women are the same, so women should be allowed in military combat roles. *Therefore, physical standards should be lowered for women to be eligible to fill combat roles in the Marines.*

Two identical cartons sit on a counter. One holds milk, and one hold spoiled milk. They are equal but not the same.

True equality means holding everyone accountable in the same way, regardless of race, gender, faith, ethnicity—or political ideology.

—Monica Crowley

Euphemism

Noun

A nicer sounding word that replaces a disliked term. *Pro-choice* is a euphemism for abortion. *Abortion* was the original euphemism for sucking a new life out of the mother's womb.

Bailout is a euphemism for crony capitalism, which can be a euphemism for *cheating*, by using power to unduly influence politicians to perform favors or using tax funds to promote business sympathetic to individual politicians' campaigns.

With the popularity of various euphemisms, meanings of words have become muddled. *Progressive* is now a popular euphemism for *communist*. It is a successful ploy to fool many Democrats and liberals into supporting totalitarianism in the guise of kindness.

Executive branch

Noun

The branch of government responsible for enacting, supporting, and enforcing the laws made by the legislative branch and interpreted by the judicial branch. The president sits at the helm of the executive branch, which includes his cabinet of secretaries, under which many regulatory agencies reside.

Article II, Section 3, of the of the Constitution states that the president "shall take care that the laws be faithfully executed." This was included to restrain the president from changing or canceling laws he didn't agree with. President Obama, a constitutional lawyer, must have been absent the day his class covered Article II because he acted as if it didn't apply to him, as evidenced in his bold and arrogant assertions:

> Wherever and whenever I can take steps without legislation to expand opportunity for more American families, that's what I'm going to do.
> Whenever Congress refuses to act, Joe and I, we're going to act.
> We're not just going to be waiting for legislation. . . . I've got a pen and I've got a phone. And I can use that pen to sign executive orders and take executive actions and administrative actions that move the ball forward.

Obama's poorly crafted Affordable Care Act imploded and revealed his empty promises, so he unilaterally changed it. Over 20 times, he changed a standing law instead of enforcing it.

Obama used his pen to sign executive orders granting millions of illegal aliens amnesty, after citing the Constitution several times during his first term to assert that he was powerless to do so.

In an attempt to enact gun control, he instructed the Bureau of Alcohol, Tobacco, Firearms and Explosives to regulate ammunition. Congress wasn't interested in making the World Wide Web a public utility, so Obama dialed the Federal Communications Commission to override Congress with a regulatory plan.

Concern about executive overreach is partisan neutral. Both parties should adhere to the boundaries set forth in the Constitution. As law professor Jonathon Turley (who voted for Obama) testified before the House Judiciary Committee, "There has been a massive gravitational shift of authority to the Executive Branch that threatens the stability and functionality of our tripartite system."

When the leader of a democratic republic ignores the legislative branch, refuses to enforce laws, and uses his or her executive branch to hand down decrees on state and local governments, private businesses, and individual citizens, he or she is not moving the ball forward, as Obama claimed, he's hurling it backward, toward the days of the autocratic crown.

Face diaper

Noun

Refers to the mask-type facial covering advocated by, strangely, the same folks who seek to limit freedom of speech. Coincidence? I think not . . .

Fake news

Noun

False information masquerading as journalism. The term "fake news" exploded into common vernacular just before the 2016 presidential election, but it's been around for over a hundred years. Though there's nothing new about spreading lies, the words have become a pejorative to discount and discredit any news story that departs from the disclaimant's agenda. Fake news has become a catch-all phrase that a nonthinker will throw at something they'd rather not consider.

It wasn't always this way. In 2017, Trump told a CNN reporter "You're fake news." He then proceeded to use Alinsky's tactics of target, isolate, and ridicule to marginalize CNN, which polarized the media—not that it wasn't quite polarized already. If you're a leftist, hating conservatives and wanted them to die horrible, slow deaths are just a Sunday morning to you. A little fake news is breakfast for the day.

What Trump successfully managed was highlighting the leftist media's bias in their reporting. If Donald Trump walked on water, the headline would read "Trump Can't Swim!"

Although the term has been diluted from overuse and misuse, it is still highly effective.

Fascism

Noun

A nationalistic or authoritative system of government and social organization.

Fascism is unlimited state power governing and dominating every aspect of life: the economy, education, media, courts, religion, health, and even our words. Some regimes use brute force (Nazi Germany), while others excessively regulate and manipulate to achieve what they claim is the common good (Franco's Spain).

> *Fascism is not defined by the number of its victims, but by the way it kills them.*
>
> —Jean-Paul Sartre

It's regularly said by liberal propagandists that conservatives are fascists seeking to impose endless rules and control our lives. Such statements are oxymoronic—stress the moronic. The fundamental aspect of fascism is a vast, controlling state. The core of conservative philosophy is limited, restrained government. It is impossible to hold a conservative view of the role of government and be a fascist. The two words are at complete odds with one another.

Comparing conservatism to fascism stems from the fact that Nazi Germany fought the communists of leftist Russia. However, the Nazis being a tad right of the communists does not make them conservatives.

The comparison also exists due to the Left labeling the Right as racist, bigoted American flag wavers. They then point to racist, genocidal nationalistic Nazi Germany as an example of fascism, and out comes an unfounded, irrational, hateful accusation predicated on a false premise.

Even if conservatives were racist, it would not follow that they are fascists. Nazi Germany was fascist, but not because it was racist, rather because the state dictated and controlled institutions and individuals. Anyone who declares that conservatism leads to fascism is ignorant of both conservatism and fascism.

In truth, fascism is leftist rather than rightist. Italian dictator Benito Mussolini summed up fascism with "Everything in the state, nothing outside the state." Fascism: the state as religion.

Sold as an effort to unify, it is really a destruction of liberty because it is the state alone that defines what "unification" involves. If an individual's opinion, religion, or business does not adhere to the dictates, then it is deemed unacceptable and quashed. The leftists in America have embraced this approach in their attempts to limit speech by enacting speech codes at universities, demonizing those who support traditional marriage, question the validity of climate change, or correctly determine a person's gender biologically.

I believe that political correctness can be a form of linguistic fascism, and it sends shivers down the spine of my generation who went to war against fascism.

—P. D. James

Feargasm

Noun

The feeling in people who allow fear to control them, because they prefer to slink off in some kind of rationalized terror than adopt some courage and grow a pair. Also, the near-erotic climax of those who relish inciting fear in others. Used originally by famous rocker and devoted hunter Ted Nugent.

*It's easy to cause a **feargasm** in sheep.*

—Ted Nugent

Filibuster

Noun

A device used in the Senate to delay or block a bill or nomination from coming to the floor for a vote. The rules of the Senate allow a single senator, or series of senators, to extend debate on a bill or speak on any subject for any length of time unless three-fifths of the Senate vote to invoke *cloture* to end the debate.

In 2013, Senator Rand Paul spoke for almost 13 hours to block a confirmation vote on President Obama's CIA director nominee, John Brennan. Paul was seeking previously unaddressed confirmation of whether the administration would allow for drone strikes against suspected American terrorists on American soil. After the filibuster, Attorney General Eric Holder issued a letter clarifying that administration policy would not allow for that. It was reassuring to learn there were some limits on the president's power!

Filibusters can be very theatrical and evoke both feelings of antagonism for slowing the wheels of government or a romanticized view of the people's representatives standing on principles, as wonderfully captured in the film *Mr. Smith Goes to Washington*, where Jimmy Stewart speaks for 23 hours against government corruption.

The filibuster is an effective tool not only in use but also in threat. Often simply a threat to filibuster a bill will send it back to committee for modification or, sometimes, to its death. Presidents have withdrawn nominations of justices, secretaries, and other officials when faced with a warning they will be held up by a filibuster.

Filibusters are always controversial. Democratic Senator Strom Thurmond's 24-hour-and-18-minutes filibuster against the Civil Rights Act of 1957 failed to thwart the bill; it passed the very next day. Thurmond's rhetorical marathon raised the arguments of opposition to civil rights, and the people did not agree. Though Thurmond filibustered for over 24 hours straight, We the People had the final word.

#Filibuster, #SenateRules

First Amendment

Noun

The U.S. Constitution was a hard-fought document that delineates the powers reserved to our government. But that wasn't enough for John Adams. No. He insisted, over strong objections by Thomas Jefferson and others, the we also ratify a Bill of Rights to specifically protect each citizen's personal civil liberties such that the government would be prevented from infringing upon them. Well, Adams was a very clever man! He saw the day coming when government overreach might attempt to deprive the citizens of more than just their money! Luckily, under withering criticism, he stood his ground, and so, now, rather than argue about whether the government should allow people to speak their minds (the bulwark of a functioning free society) or should permit prayer at all (or freedom of thought), we have the protection of the First Amendment, which reads:

> Congress shall make no law respecting an establishment of religion, or prohibiting the free exercise thereof; or abridging the freedom of speech, or of the press, or the right of the people peaceably to assemble, and to petition the government for a redress of grievances.

So, while our government assaults us with draconian regulations and punitive taxation, we can just tell them to pound through the Bill of Rights to get to our fundamental (and uniquely American) privileges. It's concrete.

#FirstAmendment, #SecondAmendment, #BillofRights

Fourth Amendment

Noun

This is the really antiquated entry in the Bill of Rights that people often overlook, but it is still pivotal and should be studied by a citizenry that wishes to remain free!

> The right of the people to be secure in their persons, houses, papers, and effects, against unreasonable search and seizures, shall not be violated.

Back in the days before the American Revolution, the British monarch conferred his unrestricted power on his soldiers. The lobsterbacks, as the red-coated soldiers were called, could wantonly strong-arm their way into people's homes, search through their things, steal their food, and basically just have free reign, because they viewed the colonists as second-class citizens, subjects of the royal crown.

The Founders and their brethren didn't care much for that.

Useful tip: Thomas Jefferson quite transparently crafted the original Declaration of Independence as a plainly worded refutation against slavery, because the Founders held that the British crown served in the role of master to the colonists. Unfortunately, the southern states of the soon-to-be union refused to sign a document that so clearly condemned them alongside King George for that unholy practice, and our Declaration was redrafted with weaker language.

Fredocon

Noun

Minted by columnist and novelist Kurt Schlichter, the term refers to the conservatives who are stupid and weak and who channel Fredo Corleone. This second son of the mafia don in *The Godfather* was driving his father when the don was assassinated. After the killing,

Fredo, who fumbled his weapon and failed to even return fire, sat on the street and cried, rather than call any authorities. According to Mr. Schlichter, Mitt Romney is a quintessential Fredocon.

> *I can handle things! I'm smart! Not like everybody says . . . like dumb . . . I'm smart and I want respect!*
> —Fredo Corleone, *The Godfather: Part II*

Freedom

Noun

The right to think, act, and speak (morally) without fear of punishment or control. A lack of slavery and absence of a despotic government.

There are degrees of freedom within nations, some having more than others, even under authoritarian rule. For example, under dictator Fulgencio Batista, independent newspapers and radio were accessible to the people of Cuba, but when Fidel Castro's communist regime seized control, he eviscerated all freedom.

The United States of America is the first truly free nation in the world. Freedom is the foundation on which we stand. We have the freedom

- To elect the leaders that represent us
- To say and print anything we want, including criticism of the leaders we chose to elect
- To practice the religion of our choice
- From forced regulations of, or participation in, a religion
- To start a business and keep the profits
- To keep and bear arms to protect ourselves
- To own property
- From government intruding and searching our property

American freedom seems inextricably tied to our prosperity, the light that draws millions upon millions to emigrate to the United

States. However, an erosion of these freedoms is underfoot. Leaders of the Left use the guise of equality and tolerance, but make no mistake, they are seeking to demolish individual liberty. Our foundation is at risk.

America will never be destroyed from the outside. If we falter and lose our freedoms, it will be because we destroyed ourselves.

—Abraham Lincoln

We are wealthy beyond measure when we are free.

—Sam Sorbo

#Freedom, #WeThePeople

Front burner

Political term

The position in which an issue of high importance is placed, designating it as priority number one.

Bill Clinton's 1992 campaign effectively put the economy on the front burner with his slogan, "It's the economy, stupid."

After the 9/11 attacks, national security and the War on Terror took front-burner status.

The Obama administration threw everything and the kitchen sink into the pan—healthcare, immigration, minimum wage, women, race relations, education—into what one could call an "equality casserole."

The items in the pan on the front burner vary depending on the chef and what meal it is for. 2016 Republican presidential candidate Donald Trump saw that people were weary and fed up with a Congress that had not delivered on its promises. Day after day they were without food, starving for sustenance. Trump dropped a hunk of American prosperity into the pan, tossed in handfuls of pepper and fiery chiles, and then cranked up the gas. The powerful aroma has drawn in the hungry masses aching to be fed.

But will the ingredients in the pan actually be cooked? Sometimes politicians put a big slab of raw meat on display and spend years talking about the importance of the superior cut, the weight, color, and smell, but never once start cooking. Social Security and other entitlement programs have driven our country into tremendous and unsustainable debt, and despite their occasional, prominent display on the stove, they remained uncooked, growing more rancid by the day.

> *Addressing efficiency is now on the front burner of public concern.*
>
> —Norman Mineta, U.S. secretary of transportation

There was a time when issues could be prioritized, attacked, and solved one by one, but that's now almost impossible unless the *true* front-burner issue is addressed: the philosophy and ideology of our culture. Are we a nation that stands on the principles of limited government, individual liberty, Judeo-Christian values, and a free-market capitalistic society? Or are we a secular welfare state that looks to big government to serve as a savior?

Gaslighting

Originating from the Patrick Hamilton 1938 stage play *Gaslight* (and a film adaptation with Ingrid Bergman and Charles Boyer), gaslighting is the systemic manipulation of a victim to think he or she is going insane. In the play, the abusive husband slowly dims the gas lights in their home, while pretending nothing has changed, in an effort to make his wife doubt her own perceptions. When she asks him if it isn't darker, he insists she is the one who is inventing things. He asks the staff to make a loud noise with the dishes, and when she goes to investigate, everyone denies having heard a noise at all. Similarly, the media tell us destructive looting and riots are "mostly peaceful" and call them "protests" as a way of characterizing them in a positive light, while the rest of us understand they are dangerous and threatening.

Example: Dr. Oz says most American's are getting used to wearing masks. Translation: You're the only odd-ball who doesn't enjoy wearing that face diaper. Gaslighting is a way of shutting down even conversation. People won't object to anything for fear of being called a racist, bigot, or just crazy. Another example might be the fact that due to the whiteness of your skin, you are deemed irrevocably racist and forced to apologize. You correctly perceive that that judgment is, in itself, terribly racist! So you ask, "Am I crazy?" No. You're being gaslighted (or gaslit.) You're not crazy—they are.

What people believe prevails over the truth.

—Sophocles

GDP/GNP

Nouns

Gross domestic product (GDP) measures a country's yearly economic output *inside* the nation's borders, including foreign-owned businesses. Gross national product (GNP) is the economic output of all the goods and services produced by the nation's citizens, both *inside and outside* of the country. GDP is the primary measure of a nation's economic status.

A rise in GDP is one indicator of economic health, but a reported rise does not mean that the economy *is* healthy. GDP includes government spending, so when the GDP does increase, we must examine where that increase occurred. Government spending is never an indicator of good health. Government does not produce. It takes taxes or borrows. It is inaccurate to include *spending* in a statement of *product*.

The government spending portion of GDP has risen unsteadily since 1929, reaching its peak in 2010 at 36.2 percent, pulling ahead of the previous 1945 high of 35.3 percent during World War II (war always increases expenditures). The ratio of government spending to GDP, especially as the baby boomer generation retires and collects Social Security and Medicare, looks to be permanently on the rise. In light of the most recent quarantine stimulus given to citizens, we must restore our domestic production. That is, of course, unless the debt overwhelms the system and it collapses. (See **Bankruptcy**.)

We want to reduce the size of government in half as a percentage of GNP over the next 25 years. We want to reduce the number of people depending on government so there is more autonomy and more free citizens.

—Grover Norquist

Genderbread person

20th-century social term

The gender-less doll that allows children to identify their "ness" on a number of different scales, including attraction and the many different labels more specific than straight and gay, including pansexual, asexual, and possibly hypersexual. It was followed by a gender unicorn and then a gender elephant. Elephants, however, are never perceived to be confused about their gender! (See www.ItsPronouncedMetrosexual .com for an illustrative drawing.)

The scale places how one thinks about oneself on the top, promoting it as the most important. The description of gender identity attempts to use biology as its argument, claiming, "It's the chemistry that composes you (e.g., hormonal levels)." But wait, hormonal levels are indicative of the biology of the sexes. Men have more testosterone; women have more estrogen. So, if hormones are determinative, then how one *thinks* matters not. The explanation is self-refuting.

The statement "and how you interpret what that means" does not overcome the previous fact. If a woman has a womanly amount of estrogen, she interprets that as having ovaries, breasts, and a uterus, all aspects of womanhood. She has little testosterone and no physical characteristics of a man. All evidence indicates that she is a woman. Interpreting these data to mean that she's a man does not mean that she's a man; it means that there is a psychological disconnect.

Genderbread dolls do not help confused people; they encourage them to ignore their psychological issue and discourage them from discovering *why* they feel as they do and how to deal with it.

The genderbread drawing promotes a destruction of absolute truths and obliterates common sense. The overwhelming majority of children observe, feel, and know the most basic of truths—there are boys and there are girls, and they are different. For the very small percentage who are confused, this doll does not help resolve their confusion for them. And for Camel, fined for cigarettes ads targeting

children, it's sadly too late to argue that the gender-bending movement targets these vulnerable young people inside government
schools!

#GenderConfusion, #MaleAndFemale

Globalization

Noun

The integration and interdependence of global economic markets.
The use of banking, manufacturing, marketing, and distribution in
countries other than the company's nation of origin. In the age of
globalization, local producers have the ability to expand their market and profits, and consumers are given an abundance of options at
lower prices.

Some argue that globalization has kept wages down in the
United States due to companies using cheaper labor in countries like
China. Cheaper labor keeps costs lower for consumers. It has also
allowed for nations that lack resources, capital, and technology but
are rich in a labor force to grow faster and achieve higher incomes.
What the government fails to consider is that the exchange of goods
and services, otherwise known as *wealth creation*, benefits both parties, that trade helps promote the values of the foreign nation, and
that those may be antithetical to American values of life and liberty.

In light of the recent COVID-19 global crisis, we hope that
Americans might rethink our approach to sending our wealth overseas, which allows governments with hostile values to target our very
health and welfare!

Global cooling

Noun

In the 1970s, there were predictions of a worldwide drop in surface and atmospheric temperatures ushering in an ice age. It did not

happen. In the summer of 2015, a study out of Britain predicted a cooling phase lasting a few decades during this century, supporting other scientists' claims citing a decrease in solar activity as the cause.

Some use it as an argument to refute global warming; then supporters pejoratively mock them, claiming, "The data were flawed," "It was only a handful of scientists that supported it," and "It was media hype." Ironically, those are the precise arguments that refute the catastrophic anthropogenic global warming theory. (See **Global warming**.)

Why is it so easy to claim that past predictions were flawed but current global warming theories are irrefutable?

There are cooling trends, and there are warming trends. It's weather; it does change. Duh, right?

Global warming

Noun

The theory that the Earth's surface is heating up to dangerous levels, which will cause catastrophic events like droughts, hurricanes, cyclones, flooding of coastal cities due to rising oceans, and extinction of certain animal species. The theory contends that it's all due to excessive human carbon dioxide emissions, or "greenhouse gases." "Anthropogenic" means human caused, the second part of the global warming theory.

The ultimate goal of proponents is to drastically reduce the world's use of fossil fuels and coal and increase the use of renewable energy. This comes with a monstrous price to the economy. Businesses would be forced to comply with high-cost regulations to cut emissions or switch from coal to . . . soybeans?

Global warming is now often called "climate change" (see **Climate change**) because warming predictions have not panned out, and there has been a 17-year pause in rising global temperatures. Oops! Data have been ignored and manipulated, and predictions are based on estimations, assumptions, and computer models with limited capabilities.

- In 2005, the United Nations warned that there would be 50 million "climate refugees" by 2010. In the areas defined as danger zones, the population has actually grown. Oops!
- In 2007, the BBC and "climate expert" Al Gore reported that the Arctic ice caps would be melted by 2013. They increased 29 percent from 2012 to 2013. Oops!
- The Intergovernmental Panel on Climate Change (IPCC) issued a prediction in 2007 that rising temperatures would kill off animal species. They now admit that climate change has not led to any animal extinction. Oops!
- In August 2010, NASA satellite data revealed the Earth's coldest temperature recorded: −135.8 degrees. Oops!

Proponents ignore these facts and often claim that 97 percent of scientists support the global warming hypothesis. However, as reported by Canadian newspaper *The National Post*: "The number stems from a 2009 online survey of 10,257 earth scientists, conducted by two researchers at the University of Illinois. The survey results must have deeply disappointed the researchers—in the end, they chose to highlight the views of a subgroup of just 77 scientists, 75 of whom thought humans contributed to climate change. The ratio 75/77 produced the 97 percent figure that pundits now tout."

And of those 75 researchers, two of them claim that their papers do not support the global warming theory. Oops!

Die-hard proponents are either unaware of the facts or choose to ignore them. The science is not "settled," as Greta Thunberg, environmentalists, and the MSM have proclaimed. Science is rarely *settled*, and it certainly isn't something one votes on. Skeptics of apocalyptic doomsday scenarios are not "deniers," a pejorative meant to evoke holocaust deniers. Many are thoughtful, distinguished scientists with tremendous knowledge based on their analysis of the data. They argue that there are far too many uncertainties to make such broad, sweeping claims. Does the uncertainty warrant overhauling the world's economy in an effort that will result (according to these same "experts") in only miniscule changes of CO_2 levels?

Global warming is hysteria. The climate changes. Always has, always will. The most extreme and notable changes occurred prior to human existence; just watch *Ice Age*.

Meteorologists have a hard time predicting the temperature for next weekend. That we would radically change the world's economy based on limited and flawed computer predictions about the weather a century from now is ludicrous.

> *I would say that basically global warming is a non-problem.*
> —Dr. Ivar Giaever, Nobel Prize winner in Physics

#GlobalWarmingHoax, #ClimateChangeHoax, #JunkScience

Gosnell, Kermit

Person

Kermit Gosnell is an abortionist who provided late-term and partial-birth abortions at his clinic in Philadelphia.

Authorities were reportedly sickened to discover the squalid conditions of the clinic, calling it a "house of horrors." They discovered dirty medical instruments, blood-stained furniture, bottles and bags of fetuses, and baby feet stored in jars. Gosnell, himself a man of color, practiced patient segregation: white patients were shown upstairs to his office, while minority patients stayed in the filthy waiting room.

According to investigative reports posted on Lifenews.com,

> There was blood on the floor. A stench of urine filled the air.
> A flea-infested cat was wandering through the facility, and
> there were cat feces on the stairs. Semi-conscious women
> scheduled for abortions were moaning in the waiting room

or the recovery room, where they sat on dirty recliners covered with blood-stained blankets.

In 2013, Gosnell was convicted of first-degree murder of three infants and involuntary manslaughter in the overdose death of one woman. Former employees testified that he performed illegal post-24-week abortions, delivering babies that were moving, breathing, and whimpering. The monster would then "snip" the necks of the newborns to kill them.

If this comes as news to you, that's because the mainstream media considered it to be "local" news and refused to report on it, because, let's face it, he kinda made abortion look bad.

An eponymously named movie was made about America's most prolific serial killer.

#KermitGosnell, #GosnellMovie

Grassroots

Noun

The local, base, or starting level of a movement; the opposite of establishment, which is old, conventional, even worn out—more like a tree (a tired, broken, partly rotten one).

Grassroots activism defined the founding of these United States of America when a small group of the common people rose up in defiance of tyranny. Their cries for liberty were echoed in the general public, and after a time, they declared themselves to be independent of the monarchy. Such behavior was unprecedented, and it brought aggressive retaliation from the world's supreme superpower of that day, Britain. Because of the inherent truth of the words, "all men are created equal," the patriots thankfully prevailed.

Today, people knocking on doors, making phone calls, distributing signs, licking envelopes, staging and attending protests, drafting letters, circulating petitions, and speaking at local city council or school board meetings comprise the new grassroots, who endeavor to educate others about the qualities and history of liberty or the "benefits" of socialism. Think Tea Party and Bernie Bros.

Some political office holders or party leaders emerged from the conservative grassroots movements. Senators Ted Cruz and Rand Paul sought to challenge the status quo from within the establishment. Marco Rubio rose up on a tidal wave of grassroots support, only to betray it with the infamous "Gang of Eight Bill" ennobling illegal immigration. Come on. A bill called "Gang of Eight?" What was he thinking? Politicians entering the establishment sometimes become part of the problem.

The grassroots movement is aided by the Internet age, which illuminates issues and calls to action, but it also allows people to *feel* as if they are *part* of a movement (posting, tweeting, and bloviating), without actually *doing* anything. The original revolutionaries were more action oriented. For instance, for all their bluster, the Bernie Bros have had very little effect.

#WeThePeople

Green New Deal

Noun

This is a reworked economic system proposed by far-left Alexandria Ocasio-Cortez (AOC) whereby people would completely lose their freedom and their cars, and the government would shut down air traffic, trucking, and cows, due to what they call "greenhouse emissions," otherwise known as plant food and cow farts. Initially proposed to save the planet, it was met with strong criticism. AOC answered that it wasn't complete yet, but she never corrected it to anything remotely resembling sanity.

Reportedly, it would cost the taxpayers several billion dollars—but, of course, we know it would cost exactly everything, as it would be the destruction of our entire economy and put us back to the dark ages. Also, no hamburgers or ice cream (banning cows), so everyone would be really grumpy.

For some inexplicable reason, people took the former bartender-turned-politician AOC seriously. But the Green New Deal is actually a watermelon—communist red on the inside.

Unemployment is low because everyone has two jobs.

—Alexandria Ocasio-Cortez

Greenhouse effect

Noun

Originally applied to greenhouses, this is the effect of trapping in the heat via the light energy that comes through glass. Today the term describes the warming of the Earth's surface and lower atmosphere due to a "blanket" of water vapor, clouds, carbon dioxide, methane, and other minor gases.

Water vapor should have the greatest effect, but scientists cannot determine from cloud formation and shadow effects whether we get warming or cooling.

Climate change alarmists want everyone to believe that CO_2 is to blame for any temperate fluctuation. Never mind that world temperatures have been fluctuating since the creation of the Earth. According to them, carbon dioxide, *emitted by humans* via the burning of fossil fuels (petroleum, coal, and natural gas), increases the greenhouse effect, and the "science is settled."

Many factors may contribute to temperature changes on the Earth's surface, like flow patterns in the ocean and atmosphere, volcanoes, comets and asteroids, variations in the Earth's orbital patterns, and variations in the sun's output and in cosmic rays that lead to variations in cloud cover.

Princeton professor and physicist William Happer explains carbon dioxide's relation to the greenhouse effect and the results on the environment:

CO_2 really is a greenhouse gas and, other things being equal, adding CO_2 to the atmosphere by burning coal, oil, and natural gas will modestly increase the surface temperature of the earth. Other things being equal, doubling the CO_2 concentration, from our current 390 ppm to 780 ppm will directly cause about one degree Celsius warming. At the current rate of CO_2 increase in the atmosphere—about 2 ppm per year—it would take about 195 years to achieve this doubling. The combination of a slightly warmer earth and more CO_2 will greatly increase the production of food, wood, fiber, and other products by green plants, so the increased CO_2 will be good for the planet, and will easily outweigh any negative effects. Supposed calamities like the accelerated rise of sea level, ocean acidification, more extreme climate, tropical diseases near the poles, etc. are greatly exaggerated.

Unfortunately, *his* science is *not* compatible with the *other* science. The long-debunked "97 percent of scientists agree" on climate change is still in the common vernacular when the topic arises. Just say, "I'm proplant, and climate change zealots are antivegan."

#CO2isPlantFood

Grooming

Verb

The practice of preparing someone for something, often with malicious intent; for example, prostitutes and sex slaves are groomed prior to being trafficked or sold for sex. Abusers flatter, befriend, and then exploit impressionable young women, men, girls, or boys. They often encourage the youngsters to finish high school or college, give them gifts, and treat them very well over a period of months, before turning on them and forcing them, often by threats of physical violence or other retribution, to perform. Grooming renders a victim incapable of doubting their abuser. *I love you, Baby, but you're a f–ing idiot, and now you're gonna do what I tell you!*

Some would say the United States has been groomed over our recent history, from a president who lied to the American public to one who insists the country must undergo *fundamental transformation*. Why else would that be tolerated by the citizens of the greatest country in the world?

Groupthink

Noun

The innate and insecure search for alignment of thought with the collective. Psychologist Irving Janis coined the term in 1972, stating in his research:

> I use the term groupthink as a quick and easy way to refer to the mode of thinking that persons engage in when concurrence-seeking becomes so dominant in a cohesive ingroup that it tends to override realistic appraisal of alternative courses of action. Groupthink is a term of the same order as the words in the newspeak vocabulary George Orwell used in his dismaying world of 1984. In that context, groupthink takes on an invidious connotation. Exactly such a connotation is intended, since the term refers to a deterioration in mental efficiency, reality testing and moral judgments as a result of group pressures.

Groupthink is herd—think lemmings—mentality. By ridiculing questions and dissent, Groupthink thrives on fear, guilt, and suppression of opposing views. Universities create a culture of groupthink with the passage of speech codes, safe zones, trigger warnings, claims of rape culture, and refusal to allow speakers who challenge their ideologies. (See **College**.)

The most dominant tactic employed in intimidating people into silence and conformity (groupthink) is manipulation of language, which restricts people's thoughts by limiting their words.

The issue of gender (or lack thereof) is a prime example. There are now men, women, transgender men and women, gender queer, and a host of others—Facebook allows you to customize, so she-male-pan-trans-questioners can rest easy. Some universities are employing the use of gender neutral pronouns "ze," "hir," "zir," "xe," "xem," and "xyr." (Spellcheck flagged every single one of these "words," but that'll undoubtedly change soon, because supposedly there are more than 82 different pronouns, now.) Does gender not matter? Despite undeniable evidence of the physical form and DNA, we must not only tolerate but accept this belief as truth. So if a man calls himself a woman, but you call him a man, he calls you a bigot!

The term "same-sex marriage" is also an attempt to control our words and ultimately our thoughts. The very definition of marriage is a union of *man and woman*. To put "same-sex" in front of it negates the meaning of the word "marriage" itself. With the help of the U.S. Supreme Court, groupthinkers have redefined marriage to mean the union of two people who love each other.

The groupthink result: Marriage equals love, at least temporarily, and anyone who disagrees hates gay people, should be sued, and should be forced into re-education classes.

Groupthink feeds on the emotional desire to be liked and included. It intimidates and threatens in order to force conformity. It removes inquiry, evaluation, reason, and dissent. Ironically, the term "groupthink" requires one to absolutely forego *thinking*.

The show that is the sworn enemy of lying, pomposity, smugness and groupthink.

—Tucker Carlson (about his FoxNews TV program)

#GroupThink, #DoubleThink, #Orwellian

Gubernatorial

Adjective

Anything relating to the governor or governor's office. Governors are the chief executives of their state. Duties vary depending on each state's constitution, but typically they sign bills into law, act as commander-in-chief of the state's National Guard, make appointments to judicial and state offices, and may grant pardons.

Gun control

Noun

The attempt by the government to disarm the people, rendering them defenseless and easier to control. Our Second Amendment protects our right to keep and bear arms, yet gun control advocates seek to restrict and even appropriate arms.

Immediately after tragedies such as school, church, and movie theater shootings, they exploit the public's anger, sadness, and fear to push their agenda and call for more restriction. After the shooting at Sandyhook Elementary School in Newtown, Connecticut, the Obama administration and congressional Democrats introduced 10 gun control bills, although none of them would have prevented the shooting. Typically, shooters have already broken existing laws. Adding yet another will not deter them. Murder is illegal. If someone is willing to break *that* law, it's unlikely they'll adhere to a law that limits the number of rounds in a magazine.

After the 2015 shooting at Emanuel African Methodist Episcopal Church in Charleston, Obama said, "At some point we as a country will have to reckon with the fact that this type of mass violence does not happen in other advanced countries." Except in Norway. It has the highest rate of 1.888 mass shooting fatalities per million people. Or Germany, where two school shootings in 2002 and 2009 took the lives of 34 children. Or France (0.347), Finland (0.132), Switzerland (0.142), and Belgium (0.128). Since Obama misstated the fact, the United States has fallen from 8th to 11th in mass shootings, at 0.089 per million people.

While major news outlets spend endless hours covering mass shootings, rarely do they note the guns often used are *already illegal*. Also rare is media coverage of victims who successfully defend themselves from crime with their guns, while, commonly, instances where the gun was solely used or intended for self-harm are included to inflate the negative numbers. Murders committed with illegal guns are rampant in cities like Chicago, Baltimore, and Detroit—all with very strict gun laws (where the overwhelming majority of gun violence is perpetrated by gang members and drug dealers). These go largely unnoticed by our media.

Proposed measures for more gun control laws do nothing to stop criminals, who by definition break laws. They rather target law-abiding citizens seeking to protect themselves against criminals.

Gun control arguments are built on manipulation of statistics, exploitation of emotions, and outright lies. While some proponents may have pure intentions and fervently believe restricting gun ownership will decrease the amount of gun violence, belief does not equal truth and is not a valid reason for restricting or revoking an individual's constitutional right.

Laws don't stop gun violence. Law-abiding, responsible citizens with guns stop gun violence.

I have a very strict gun control policy: if there's a gun around,
I want to be in control of it.

—Clint Eastwood

#SecondAmendment, #2A, #GunRights, #GunSense

Habeas corpus

Noun

A person's right to be brought before a judge and to a fair trial in court, especially in order to be released, in the case that no proof is offered of legal wrongdoing warranting detention. Article I, Section 9, Clause 2, of the Constitution states:

> The Privilege of the Writ of Habeas Corpus shall not be
> suspended, unless when in Cases of Rebellion or Invasion
> the public Safety may require it.

It is a vital, foundational principle of our country. Dwight D. Eisenhower said:

> We are proud because from the beginning of this nation
> man can walk upright no matter who he is or who she is.
> He can walk upright and meet his friend or his enemy. . . .
> And he does not fear that, because that enemy may be in a
> position of great power . . . that he can be suddenly thrown
> in jail to rot there without charges and with no recourse to
> justice. We have the Habeas Corpus Act and we respect it.

Habeas corpus has been misinterpreted and stretched beyond the reach of its intent. The Nonhuman Rights Project brought a lawsuit on behalf of two chimpanzees at Stonybrook University on Long Island seeking to afford them legal personhood rights. The attorney for chimps Hercules and Leo argued that they were "autonomous and self-determining beings" and therefore deserved the rights of "legal persons." He also likened their confinement to slavery. In a victory for common sense, the New York State Supreme Court denied the writ of habeas corpus, and the proceeding was dismissed in July 2015.

In contrast, in 2008, the Supreme Court ruled in *Boumedien v. Bush* that the right of habeas corpus applies to terrorist detainees at Guantanomo Bay. Essentially the court ruled that jihadists seeking to murder and destroy America captured *outside* the United States and held on foreign soil have a constitutional right to challenge their detainment *inside* America. Late Justice Antonin Scalia wrote in his dissent:

> At least 30 of those prisoners hitherto released from Guantanamo Bay have returned to the battlefield. . . . It was reported only last week that a released detainee carried out a suicide bombing against Iraqi soldiers in Mosul, Iraq.

And Chief Justice John Roberts wrote:

> This statutory scheme provides the combatants held at Guantanamo greater procedural protections than had ever been afforded alleged enemy detainees—whether citizens or aliens—in our national history.

It would've made more sense and been more fitting to extend the right to the chimps than to the terrorists.

Happy warrior

Noun

Dating back to a poem, "Character of the Happy Warrior," by William Wordsworth in 1806, which describes an ideal and idealistic fighter. This phrase has inspired many metaphors in military and political campaigns—because, face it—politics is war. Andrew

Breitbart was famously a happy warrior, due to his incredible alacrity to fight while smiling at his purported enemies. He would invite those who vehemently disagreed with him to lunch. At the Anthony Weiner press conference, when Weiner himself kept the press waiting for long after he was due to speak to clear his name of the "sexting" scandal, Breitbart boldly snagged the podium to explain how the media was impugning his own reputation and exactly how Weiner would be unable to in any way justify his indiscretions. Breitbart emerged from that valiant effort the uncontested winner. Because of his own hubris (and unquestionable guilt), Weiner didn't stand a chance against happy warrior Breitbart.

> *It's fun to be liked, but when standing up for what you believe in, it's also very fun not to be liked.*
>
> —Andrew Breitbart

Hegemony

Noun

The political, economic, military, or cultural influence or authority over a group or nation.

The term is used both positively and negatively, and America has been labeled hegemonic as praise and condemnation. We most certainly are hegemonic as an *influence* on the rest of the world by our example of liberty, free-market capitalism, willingness and ability to fight evil regimes, and provision of humanitarian aid to struggling nations. However, many often use the term to condemn our leadership as domination. (See **Imperialism**.)

> *I believe—though I may be wrong, because I'm no expert—that this war is about what most wars are about: hegemony, money, power and oil.*
>
> —Dustin Hoffman

Hoffman was referring to the war in Iraq, and he really hit the nail on the head: he's no expert, and he is wrong. His use of "hegemony" was not referring to influence and leadership but was an indictment of America as imperialist. If U.S. wars are about hegemony, money, power, and oil, why doesn't the U.S. rule over Germany and Japan? Was there oil in Korea and Vietnam? The history books must've missed that tidbit.

Leftists tend to punctuate their arguments about foreign policy by accusing America of a lustful grab for power and domination. They think sounding intellectual with the use of a three-syllable, lesser-known word will add credence to their claim.

America is the antithesis (conservatives can use big words too) of the leftist view of hegemony. Hegemony is what America fights against. We do not seek to rule other nations but participate in helping them to crawl out from under domination.

America does have a great deal of power and influence and has played a huge rule in the world because it is the freest, greatest, and most successful nation on the planet. But it is not hegemonic in leftist terms. After the collapse of the Soviet Union, America did not ride in and seize Poland, the Czech Republic, and the Baltic states; it encouraged and supported them in their creation of new, free societies. Secretary of State George Schultz said of Reagan's approach:

> I recall President Reagan's Westminster speech in 1982—
> that communism would be consigned to the ash heap of
> history. And what happened? Between 1980 and 1990 the
> number of countries that were classified as free or mostly
> free increased by 50 percent. Open political systems have
> been gaining ground and there's good reason for it. They
> work better.

The United States of America exercises influence not by conquering and controlling but rather by leading and assisting.

House of Representatives

Noun

This body of government is comprised of 435 elected officials. Members are directly elected by the people, according to population data, and serve a term of two years. On the first day of every new Congress, the majority party chooses the Speaker of the House, the presiding officer of the chamber. He or she appoints members to select and conference committees and determines which committee will consider which bills.

As stated in Article I, Section 7, of the Constitution, all bills for raising revenue must originate in the House. It also has the power to impeach the president and elect the president if there is no majority in the electoral college, which occurred in 1800, when he House elected Thomas Jefferson after a tie with Aaron Burr, and in 1824, sending John Quincy Adams to the White House.

The main job of the House is in the name: representatives. They are to confer with and represent the people of their district. Sadly, this is not always the case, and members spend their time trying to keep their jobs and power rather than speaking for the people who put them in office. The best way for the people to show their dismay at a member's performance is to vote—for someone else.

Humanism

Noun

A worldview that pretends to promote human beings while proposing they are a collection of molecules and chemical reactions, evolved purely by chance, thus denying them any value. It repudiates the existence of a Divine Creator and elevates physical matter above all. Humanism states that all problems can be solved through rational problem solving.

Ironically, the notion that molecular machines employ rational problem solving is incredibly *irrational*. Human reason itself refutes the idea of chance-based evolution. Even atheist, evolutionary biologist J. B. S Haldane acknowledges the self-refuting nature of materialistic humanism:

> If my mental processes are determined wholly by the
> motions of atoms in my brain, I have no reason to suppose
> that my beliefs are true . . . and hence I have no reason for
> supposing my brain to be composed of atoms.

And what challenges require solutions in a world where there is no right or wrong or good or evil? Good and evil are not material entities; thus they must be opinions. But opinions are not made up of physical matter. Nor is love, beauty, justice, or morality.

If there is no absolute morality or truth, then all is permissible, and there is no need for justice. Who decides that theft, rape, and murder are bad and should be punished? Molecules? Atoms? This is not to say that humanists can't be good or moral, but if they claim that Mother Theresa was good and Ted Bundy was bad, they cannot use humanism as the basis for their argument.

Humanists assert their philosophy as true, offering explanations for their belief in materialism through the use of nonmaterial reason (flawed, though it may be). Therefore, any argument a humanist makes for his or her philosophy is in fact an argument *against* it.

Twitter supplied the perfect example: "#Humanism because God is imaginary."

What proton, neutron, electron, or physical element supplied the ability to conjure up an unseen deity of love and forgiveness? What material prompted someone to even envision the concept of love and forgiveness? A more logical tweet would be "#God because humanism does not allow for imagination."

#Logic101, #StealingFromGod

Humble brag

Noun

False humility. Some say this phrase originated in the 1700s, while others believe it's more current. Nonetheless, the speaker tries to appear unpretentious and modest while engaging in shameless self-promotion. "Yikes! I accidentally just butt-dialed Tom Hanks! Ugh," tweeted the guy who wants you to know he's got Hanks' number. There's other kinds that happen in conversation: "I love this famous YouTuber's video!" "Yeah. He sent me that one before he posted it."

Hypocrite

Noun

An individual who claims to believe one thing but acts contrary to his or her statements, kinda like the person who says, "Do what I say, not what I do."

An example of blatant hypocrisy is the Obamacare act, which Congress approved while exempting themselves from its edicts. Another good one is democrat political leaders forbidding public gatherings because of COVID-19, but approving of protesting and rioting. Hypocrites don't abide by their own quarantine rules. Chris Cuomo clandestinely broke his well-publicized quarantine to visit his new construction project in the Hamptons, but he got caught— so he blamed the guy who caught him! Neil Ferguson, the director of the Abdul Latif Jameel Institute for Disease and Emergency Analytics (J-IDEA) and director of the MRC Centre for Global Infectious Disease Analysis, devised the entire lock-down strategy. Then he impetuously snuck out for a secret tryst with his married mistress.

According to the Daily Caller, "CNN reporters like Kaitlin Collins obsess over masks when the cameras are on, but when they think they're off, off comes their masks!" Al Gore and Hollywood elites lecture the world about carbon footprints while flying around the globe on private jets and directing their personal drivers to idle their SUVs in the cold so they are warm when they get in, after their meetings to discuss saving the planet from the climate catastrophe. Finally, Hillary Clinton put the *H* in hypocrisy by accusing Trump of being in bed with the Russians, after making shady deals with them herself and publicly presenting them with her infamous "reset button." But there's a final piece that really drives the point home: "In late July 2016, U.S. intelligence agencies obtained insight into Russian intelligence analysis alleging that U.S. Presidential candidate Hillary Clinton had approved a campaign plan to stir up a scandal against U.S. Presidential candidate Donald Trump by tying him to Putin and the Russians' hacking of the Democratic National Committee," according to TownHall.com. So Clinton hypocritically called out Trump for his (imagined) proximity and friendliness toward Russia, after her own courtship with them, and she's the one who *originated rumors of his so-called bromance with Putin?*

Yes, it takes skill to be such an outrageous but effective liar, and the hypocrisy brings deceit to a whole new level.

> *No. We just can't trust the American people to make those types of choices. . . . Government [made up of American people] has to make those choices for people.*
>
> —Hillary Clinton

Ideology

Noun

A comprehensive vision of how one views society and his or her role in it. Ideology is a set of standards, principles, ethics, and doctrines within a group, class, religion, or political party determining what they believe and how they behave.

Ideologues are slaves to ideology, refusing to consider any view outside that established set of beliefs. Blinded by their overall worldview, they ignore or discredit evidence that conflicts with their ideology.

Leftism, progressivism, and even socialism are ideologies that may seem well intentioned in their desire to create a land of equality, but deeper inside the hallways of academia, Hollywood, and journalism, one finds unacceptable methods of achieving the results. They require government-controlled education, healthcare, school lunches, assaults on religion, moral relativism, and stripping individuals of rights—all done under the guise of optimistic phrases like "The New Deal," "The Great Society," and "Fundamental Transformation."

Concepts may be attractive, but the devil is always in the details when dealing with ideology.

#ConfirmationBias

Idiot

Noun

A fool, a person who is profoundly stupid or incapable of reasoning. Typically, anyone with a *D* next to their name on the news.

In the recent coronavirus crisis, the leftist U.S. mainstream media initially conspired to prevent any blame from falling on China (and consequently their beloved Chinese Communist Party), and they ran a campaign to promote China as having been the most responsible of all the nations in both dealing with the crisis and managing their own citizens. Never mind that, allowing international travel to continue to and from Wuhan, China, deliberately put the rest of the world at risk for three weeks, after shutting down *domestic travel* for Wuhan. After President Trump instituted the travel ban prohibiting flights from China to the United States (January 31, 2020), the leftists in the United States encouraged folks to go to Chinatown (Pelosi—February 24) and enjoy the Chinese New Year parade (De Blasio—February 9). Then, of course, they blamed Trump for not acting fast enough, because truth has no sway to an idiot.

Even Bill Gates praised China's initial efforts and downplayed how they knowingly deceived the rest of the world: "I don't think that's a timely thing because it doesn't affect how we act today." It sure better, or we all become the idiots we are discussing now.

Leftists try to claim they are scientific, while they actively deny science, as in the case of global climate change, which used to be known as global cooling before they made it global warming. Neither of those panned out, but did they just stop making stuff up? No! They doubled down and still claim the world is ending in 12 years. Does it remind you of Chicken Little and "The sky is falling!"? Of course. He was an idiot, and so are they.

Finally, there is the term "useful idiot," supposedly coined by Vladimir Lenin and/or Joseph Stalin to describe those ideologues who supported communism without understanding it. Used for the press and politicians. To be a useful idiot, you must be twice as stupid, because you are enthusiastically signing your own death warrant.

If you've got a better word for reality deniers and situational inventors, I'd love to hear it.

It is better to be silent and be thought a fool than to speak and remove all doubt.

—Unknown

It is better to educate oneself through open exploration than refuse to learn and be taught the hard way.

—Sam Sorbo

Immigration

Noun

A permanent move to a foreign country. Traditionally, immigrants came to America for freedom, opportunity, and economic prosperity, traditionally known as "The American Dream." They learned English, changed their names to sound less "ethnic," and otherwise culturally endeavored to become Americans.

My, how the times have changed! Now, many don't make an effort to learn English, instead clinging to the culture of the country they fled and insisting that Americans cater to it. They do not wish to integrate and become Americans. They wish to *benefit from* America while rebuking her in the same breath.

The United States accepts one million legal immigrants a year, and who really knows how many *illegal* ones? Official reports maintain that there are currently 11 million illegal immigrants in the United States, based on Census data, which are unreliable at best when dealing with lawbreakers. It is also an outdated figure.

Currently, law enforcement detains illegals as they cross the border. Then they release them with a hearing date, to which no one in his or her right mind would show up (90 percent don't!).

Wanting to secure our southern border, enforce the law, and keep out criminals is not anti-immigrant or racist, as some claim. It's protection and self-preservation. The U.S. immigration system is outdated, broken, and does not serve our economic, security, or overall national interests. Consider:

- Forty-five percent of illegals entered the United States legally and overstayed their visa.
- Immigrants have sent more than $120 billion a year back to their home countries, weakening the American economy.
- In 2013, the Obama administration released 36,007 criminal immigrants with 88,000 convictions, including murder, kidnapping, and sexual assault. In 2014, another 30,558 with only 79,059 criminal convictions. (Pop the champagne; a few hundred less murders, kidnappers, and rapists were released!)
- Sixty-two percent of illegal immigrant households in America and 49 percent of legal immigrants use at least one form of welfare. This rises to 72 percent when measuring immigrant households with children.
- In 2014, President Obama issued executive amnesty providing five million illegals (maybe more) Social Security numbers, photo IDs, and work permits allowing them to "legally" take jobs from American citizens during a time of high unemployment and low wages.

Stopping illegal immigration would mean that wages would have to rise to a level where Americans would want the jobs currently taken by illegal aliens.

—Thomas Sowell

Activists and employers make strange bedfellows, but the two have hopped into the sack to serve their cause. The former wants more voters for the Democratic Party, the latter, cheap labor. Take, for instance, the agricultural industry with its plea for more workers. Farm work is a low-skilled job with no educational requirement. There are 30 million working-age American citizens with only a high school education who are unemployed. Increasing wages and improving working conditions would attract these native citizens, but instead the industry keeps wages low by importing poverty. Sixty-seven percent of head of household farm workers are on some form of welfare. There are 361,000 school-age children in the households that pay little, if any, taxes. They come nowhere near covering the cost they create.

America has a history of robust immigration that has positively affected the nation. More immigrants have come to America seeking freedom than to all other nations of the world combined. It is a welcoming nation that provides the opportunity for life, liberty, and the pursuit of happiness. But we are also a nation of laws and principles, and those who want to be a part of the country must abide by its laws and embrace its principles.

As it says on the Statue of Liberty, America *is* a beacon for the tired, poor, and huddled masses yearning to be free. Free, as in liberty. Not yearning to collect free healthcare, education, and food stamps. And not free to commit crime.

#Immigration, #ImmigrationReform, #AnchorBabies, #NoAmnesty, #SecureTheBorders

Imperialism

Noun

The systematic push of one country's cultural, economic, and political viewpoints on a weaker one by diplomatic or military force. Imperialists exert authority and control, as in a hostile takeover

Britain is the most notable of imperialist nations, having colonized areas in every corner of the world. The peak of British imperialism was captured in the phrase, "The sun never sets on the British Empire." Britain controlled, among others, India, African nations, Caribbean islands, and the colonies of America. It seized the resources of the areas, enslaved their inhabitants, controlled their economies, and established the sovereignty of the British crown.

The idea that America is imperialist began percolating in the bongs of the hippie movement of the 1960s. Protestors claimed the war in Vietnam was about American imperialism but never bothered to explain what resources the United States was seeking, the people we were enslaving, or the enterprises we began controlling. They somehow missed that we were fighting *against* the North Vietnamese, who were murderous imperialists toward South Vietnam.

Those idiot hippies' legacy remains in today's leftists, who called the U.S. involvement in Afghanistan imperialism. *Insert eye-roll here.* Fighting terrorist mentality (stoning rape victims, throwing men off rooftops for being gay, genital mutilation of little girls), while building schools and emancipating women from the walking prison (burka) is *not* imperialism.

When earthquakes, droughts, and disease strike impoverished nations, America shows up to help. When there are evil tyrants to be fought, America shows up. Delivering vital necessities to impoverished countries, overthrowing tyrants, and helping free the oppressed are not imperialism. They are simply humanitarian.

Incentive

Noun

The very thing that motivates a person to do anything; a reward or gain worthy of output. It is why children try harder in school to achieve better grades, valedictorian status, and acceptance to a university. Incentive is why free-market capitalism works. A better job, a higher wage, respect, and recognition: these are incentives. Removing incentives destroys ambition and quality.

> *An incentive is a bullet, a key: an often tiny object with astonishing power to change a situation.*
>
> —Steven D. Levitt, author of *Freakonomics*

Incumbent

Noun

An official currently in office. Used in reference to elections when the candidate seeks to be reelected.

An incumbent typically has advantages over his or her opponent: name recognition, funding resources, campaign-team structure, and experience. House incumbents have won 85 percent of their races for the past 50 years and Senate incumbents 82 percent of the time since 1964.

However, incumbency can also be a noose around the neck of a candidate when the people are fed up with the status quo of government. In 2014, incumbent House Majority Leader Eric Cantor lost the primary election for his seat in Congress. Republican voters in Virginia sent a message that they would no longer stand for "business as usual," that Cantor had betrayed them on the immigration issue, and that he no longer represented the people.

Though there are instances when incumbents are voted out, it's generally a strength because despite Cantor's exit and Congress having an extremely low approval rating, almost 95 percent of incumbents won reelection in 2014.

#Incumbents, #TermLimits, #VoteThemOut

Ineptocracy

Noun

A system of government where those least capable of producing elect those least able to lead to secure goods and services by confiscating wealth from the most able (but diminishing in number) producers to surrender to those least worthy of receipt. (See also **Socialism**.) In some instances, skillful people feel compelled to signal their approval for this system of government, but that still don't make it right or successful.

Infidel

Noun

A person who does not adhere to a particular faith or religion; commonly used by Muslims to describe Christians, Jews, Hindus, Buddhists, atheists, or, more simply put, every non-Muslim on Earth.

> *Hamas cannot make peace with the Israelis. That is against what their God tells them. It is impossible to make peace with infidels, only a ceasefire.*
>
> —Mosab Hassan Yousef

In Islam, there is Muslim and there is infidel, and only the former has value as a human being.

Islam

Religion

A monotheistic religious, legal, and political system, based on the Quran, which Muslims claim to be the undisputed holy revelation to the prophet Muhammad, the Hadith, and the Sunnah. (See also **Sharia law**.) There are approximately 1.4 billion Muslims worldwide.

In a world where numerous heinous acts of terror are committed by followers of Islam but political correctness dominates, there has been a painstaking effort to find the right adjective, prefix, or suffix to exhibit "tolerance":

- Moderate Islam
- Fundamentalist Islam
- Radical Islam
- Islam Extremism
- Islamist

These descriptions are very ugly. It is offensive and an insult to our religion. There is no moderate or immoderate Islam. Islam is Islam, and that's it.

—Recep Tayyip Erdogan, president of Turkey

Erdogan's statement represents those who reject the idea that the doctrine and goal of Islam are malleable. Though there are some Muslims who do not wish to live under the rule of Sharia or impose it on non-Muslims, how does one tell the difference? "Islamist" most accurately describes the belief system that Islam is the comprehensive guide regulating *all* elements of life that should be implemented and enforced worldwide. Muslim Brotherhood founder Hassan al-Banna used it to refer to all believers who desire and support the goal of establishing Sharia-controlled societies regardless of whether or not they *actively* engage in violent means themselves.

For hundreds of millions of Muslims, Islam is not principally about the individual. It is about the umma, the Muslim nation. It is at least as focused on dominance in this world as on salvation in the next.

—Andrew C. McCarthy

Insurgents

Noun

People who rise against a government regime in revolt against authority, usually in an armed resistance.

After the removal of Iraqi dictator Sadaam Hussein, the United States aided the people of Iraq in establishing a stable and representative government. Insurgent terrorist groups sought an Islamic-run state and attempted to stop the democratization. Ultimately, they were defeated when the United States sent a surge of forces in 2007. The counterinsurgency required an upping of military troops to fight and train the Iraqi army, but it also strongly focused on restoring the economy and building a new political infrastructure.

Internationalism

Noun

The view that nations should join together to address and form consensus on issues of economics, culture, and security. On its face, it sounds like a nice kumbaya idea, but it becomes more problematic when influence and authority are given to nations that are, in fact, threats to world security.

The United Nations is the prime example of internationalism by valuing each nation equally, which indirectly undermines America's identity and patriotism. The internationalism philosophy condemns the idea that America is exceptional and even labels it dangerous. It obfuscates America's leadership role in freeing millions from oppression and lifting millions out of poverty, and our participation as host undermines our sovereignty by ignoring that lacking a strong identity, national pride, and unique principles leads to an unwillingness to protect and defend our nation.

UN members are not democratically elected.

Russia is a permanent member of the UN Security Council that "has primary responsibility, under the UN Charter, for the maintenance of international peace and security." How exactly does Russia—the nation that seized Crimea and militarily occupies the sovereign nation of Ukraine—help maintain international peace and security?

These are UN past and current appointments:

- Libya (a state sponsor of terrorism)—Chair of Human Rights Commission
- North Korea—Nuclear Disarmament Commission
- China—Human Rights Council
- Iran—Commission on the Status of Women

- Syria—Security Council
- Saudi Arabia—Head of Consultative Group of Human Rights Council

Over half the members of the United Nations are not democracies but rather subvert liberty and engage in atrocities. The notion that this is a wise, discerning body capable of addressing such vital issues as safety, security, and human rights is preposterous. At the United Nations, the nuts truly are running the asylum.

Internationalism places world opinion and international law over values and morality. Many who opposed the Iraq War argued that it was illegal because the United Nations didn't authorize it. The fact that Iraq was under the rule of despotic tyrant Sadaam Hussein did not concern them. It never would, because it's tough to make the argument that Russia, China, and France are the best judges on whether a war is necessary, moral, or just. The first two are authoritarian human rights violators, and the third laid down the red carpet when Nazi Germany came a knockin'.

America is guided by principled morality; the international community is not. To grant it ultimate authority is foolish and dangerous.

Patriotism is usually stronger than class hatred, and always stronger than internationalism.

—George Orwell

Irreligion

Noun

The combination of agnosticism and atheism. Wikipedia added irreligion to its list of world religions as the indifference to, rejection of, or simple absence of religion and then says that 16 percent of the world is irreligious. That's a ruse, though, because it's just their way to impose some group identity on everyone, and grouping undecideds with atheists just makes atheists seem more popular than they really are.

Agnosticism is just delaying thought, as if any decision is unnecessary. But your worldview colors all your perceptions and your actions, so religion (worldview) is the most important research, study, and decision you can make in life. Therefore, irreligion, or the reluctance to decide, is actually a decision for secular humanism, masquerading as apathy. And secular humanism has killed, via its political expression of communism, more than 100 million people in the recent 100 years. (See **Secular humanism**.)

That's an interesting club to decide to join, whether purposely or accidentally.

ISIS

Noun

Terrorists calling themselves the Islamic State of Iraq and Syria. It's also known as ISIL (Islamic State in the Levant). They seek to establish world domination through mass murder and genocide. They have established a caliphate in Syria and Iraq and have a stronghold in North and Western Africa. In total, they control an area larger than the United Kingdom.

ISIS has proven themselves to be the most foul, barbaric, and evil of terrorists by proudly displaying their heinous acts of beheading, crucifying, burning people alive, drowning people in cages, raping women and children, and selling them into sex slavery.

Once called the "J.V. [junior varsity] team" by Barack Obama, the funding and reach of ISIS are beyond any past terrorist organization. They are a military force tens of thousands strong, taking in millions of dollars a day, funded by oil sales, smuggling, extortion, and kidnapping ransoms. They denounce the Western lifestyle but exploit the most illustrative element of it: social media. Through the use of Internet propaganda, they are successfully expanding their reach and threat by manipulating and grooming young minds and recruiting fellow barbarians across Europe and the United States.

ISIL is as sophisticated and well-funded as any group that we have seen. They're beyond just a terrorist group. They marry ideology, a sophistication of strategic and tactical military prowess. They are tremendously well-funded. Oh, this is beyond anything that we've seen. So we must prepare for everything.

—Chuck Hagel

Jingoism

Noun

Extreme nationalism or patriotism pursued through aggressive foreign policy and war. It is a derogatory term used to criticize America's military actions.

Some equate it with pride and love of country. *New York Times* op-ed columnist Charles M. Blow wrote:

> [S]ometimes, America requires critique. Jingoism is an avoidance of realism. You can simultaneously love and be disappointed in the object of your love, wanting it to be better than it is. In fact, that is a measure of love. Honest critique is a pillar of patriotism.

Blow was writing about America's imperfections and the right to critique it and had the audacity to apply the word "jingoism" in reference to conservatives who respect and desire to preserve the foundations of the country. Either he doesn't know what the word means, or he believes patriotism means, "I love war. Let's go to war with everyone." Either way, it is he who avoids realism and he who is not using honest critique.

In reference to actual war, those on the left use it selectively. They apply it to Republican presidents George H. W. Bush in the first Gulf War and George W. Bush in the second. However, Democrat Harry Truman was not a jingoist for entering the Korean War, nor was Lyndon Johnson during the Vietnam War. Although, curiously, Republican Richard Nixon was for that exact same war.

Jingoism is rhetoric used to demonize patriotic Americans who think their country is exceptional, moral, and freedom loving and who think the flag representing all those things should be waved, not burned.

Judaism

Religion

A religion based on the Torah (the first five books of the Old Testament) and the writings of the prophets that believes God is supernatural, personal, good, and holy. It gave birth to the world's first ethical monotheism. Only from *one* God can come *one* code of morality, and that is the essence of Judaism. Unlike Christianity, where salvation is gained through the grace of Jesus Christ, Judaism holds that God judges man by his behavior and works.

> God has told you what is good and what God requires of
> you only that you act justly, love goodness and walk humbly
> with your God. (Micah 6:8)

There are three main branches of Judaism:

- Orthodox—believes in the divine inspiration of the Old Testament and upholds the Talmud (rabbinic teachings) as authoritative on interpretation of Jewish law.
- Conservative—practices the traditions and laws but does so through conservative adaptation to contemporary culture.
- Reform—considers the teachings and laws outdated. It focuses on ethical teachings but does not believe in divine revelation or a messianic hope.

Judaism should not be confused with the term "Jewish," which can mean religiosity *or* ethnicity. There are many agnostic, atheist, and Christian Jews. They may be ethnically Jewish, but they do not practice the religion of Judaism.

Judicial branch

Noun

The federal court system outlined in Article III of the Constitution. It established the U.S. Supreme Court and allowed for Congress to establish the lower federal court system. Justices in both arenas are appointed and serve for life. Section 2 of Article III outlines the powers of the Court: to settle disputes between states, between states and the federal government, and between citizens of different states.

The majority of Supreme Court cases involve ruling on constitutionality. However, this is not a power designated to it in the Constitution. The Supreme Court gave itself this power in *Marbury v. Madison* and reinforced it in *Cooper v. Aaron*, arguing that *Marbury* established "the basic principle that the federal judiciary is supreme in the exposition of the law of the Constitution." This flies in the face of the system of checks and balances. The court established itself and its interpretations as the supreme law of the land and the final word. The legislative and executive branches—which are designated to uphold and support the Constitution—have no recourse to challenge or correct the directives handed down from the high holy bench.

The justices are adjudicating based on social views and personal opinions rather than law. They are rationalizing rulings by arguing that the Constitution is "living" and malleable to suit societal and cultural changes. To place personal interpretation above what the Constitution actually *says* is not jurisprudence is activism.

One of the most egregious and consequential rulings of the U.S. Supreme Court was the 1973 decision in *Roe v. Wade*. The ruling forced the legalization of abortion in all states, usurping states' rights to make their own laws regarding the issue. The Court ruled invoking the due process and equal protection clauses of the 14th Amendment. The amendment was clearly written to protect citizens from government abuses that deprive them of life, liberty, and property without fair process. The part about a right to kill an unborn baby must be written in invisible ink that only they can read.

The Court also cited previous cases that established a broad "right to privacy." Once again, not found in the Constitution. And even if it were, killing a baby has nothing to do with privacy. The Court did not uphold the Constitution; it added to it. It *made up* a "right."

In 2014, it again invoked the once-size-fits-all 14th Amendment in *Obergefell v. Hodges* when it magically found the "right" for same-sex couples to marry under the equal protection clause. The 14th Amendment was written in response to the Civil War. It was to address the rights of newly freed slaves who previously had no protection under the law. It had nothing to do with marriage. Marriage is never once mentioned in the Constitution.

In the history of humanity, marriage has never been anything other than the union between a man and woman—it is the *definition* of marriage. To modify the word with "gay" or "same sex" negates the meaning of the word. There is no such thing as gay *marriage*. Therefore, it is impossible for an amendment to protect something that does not exist. The court, once again, *made up* a "right" to create a law in order to promote "social justice." None of which is within their purview.

The Court slammed down a double whammy in both *Roe v. Wade* and *Obergefell v. Hodges*. It rewrote the Constitution, creating "rights" that do not exist, and then stomped all over states' rights by forcing them to comply, despite the will of the people of the state. Of course, many of the states had already spit on the will of the people by fellow judicial activist brothers-in-arms at state court levels who overturned voter-passed legislation to keep the definition of marriage as between a man and a woman.

Junta

Noun

A military group running a country after seizing control in a coup d'état, ousting what they claim to be a corrupt civilian government.

Often claiming the desire to create or restore stability and peace, they generally seize control in a bloodbath and proceed to implement authoritarian measures.

Latin America has a long history of corruption and chaos, and many countries have spent many years under harsh junta rule. Most notably was Argentina from 1976 to 1983, when 30,000 people were murdered. Other nations under the control of brute military force were Chile, Guatemala, Bolivia, Paraguay, and Uruguay.

Africa is another part of the world quite familiar with coups ending in military rule: Sierra Leone, Gambia, and Central African Republic. Some eventually pave the way to form a version of democracy, but often once the junta are in control, they rig elections in their favor and install a president who complies with the military's orders.

Jus ad bellum

Noun

Latin for "right to war," it is the set of criteria referred to before engaging in war. The measures by which a nation determines if the war is just. Commonly held standards are

- Just cause: defense against aggression
- Just intent: establish freedom and peace
- Waged by legitimate authority: government, state (not individuals)
- Reasonable chance at success
- Proportionality: sufficient but not excessive force
- A last resort

"War. Huh. Good God, ya'all. What is it good for?" Singer Edwin Starr tows the leftist line answering the question with, "Absolutely nothing." Really? Nothing? The Civil War wasn't good for freeing the slaves? World War II wasn't necessary to stop the slaughter of millions of Jews and Hitler's takeover of Europe?

Another line from his song is, "Oh war, I despise. Because it means the destruction of innocent lives." He neglects to mention the innocent lives that war *saves*. His entire song is a simplistic notion that gained momentum during the Vietnam War and many still cling to today.

People who use the bumper sticker, "War is not the answer," do so without asking questions. Will war topple a tyrant? Will it provide justice and spread freedom? Will it defend and save lives? War is messy and tragic, but sometimes it *is* the answer, and jus ad bellum is a moral framework to determine if or when it is necessary to achieve the greater good.

> *War is an ugly thing, but not the ugliest of things: the decayed and degraded state of moral and patriotic feeling which thinks nothing worth a war, is worse. . . . A man who has nothing which he is willing to fight for, nothing which he cares more about than he does about his personal safety, is a miserable creature who has no chance of being free, unless made and kept so by the exertions of better men than himself.*
>
> —John Stuart Mill

KAG

Acronym

The acronym for "Keep America Great"—the newer, revised slogan for the Donald J. Trump for president campaign. (See **MAGA**.)

#KAG, #Trump, #KeepAmericaGreat

Karen

Noun

Originally emanating from a viral video of an altercation between a store clerk who carelessly called a trans customer "Sir," the "Karen" term applies to people who are emotionally fragile, aggressive, and narcissistic. Karens insist on getting their way and will scream, throw tantrums, and even resort to violence, as in the case of the woman in Manhattan Beach who dumped her hot coffee on a gentleman eating a burrito outside a coffee shop because in conversation he confessed he didn't believe in masks. She later attacked him and ripped his shirt because he refused to bow to her mask god. Other covidiots have done far worse damage to property and life, prompting the Left to begin efforts to brand conservatives as pejorative for refusing to wear a mask. See how childish leftists are?

> *I know you are, but what am I?*
> —Unknown Karen to the world at large

#Covidiot, #CovidKaren, #Karen, #Covid19

Keynesian economics

Noun

A theory devised by economist John Maynard Keynes (1883–1946), who believed that government intervention and stimulus spending are the only ways to solve a depression. When economic shock leaves demand below potential supply, people stop spending, and businesses slow production. Consequently, the circle of falling demand and production shrinks the economy. Keynesian advocates believe government spending can increase demand and production by injecting "new money" into the economy.

It does not work. It did not work in the 1930s New Deal when lawmakers doubled federal spending and the unemployment rate remained over 20 percent. It did not work in 1990s Japan when the government passed 10 stimulus bills over eight years, and their economy remained sluggish. Nor did it work in 2008 when President George W. Bush issued a round of tax rebates in an attempt to curb a recession that only continued to worsen. Again, under Obama, the $835 billion stimulus seemed to have little impact in boosting the economy, as America experienced its most anemic recovery in history, but it doubled as a way for Obama to bet on businesses with taxpayer money (all of which failed):

- Solyndra—$535 million
- A123 Systems—$749 million
- Abound—$400 million
- Evergreen Solar—$527 million
- Ener1—$118 million

Under Trump, the COVID relief checks go directly to consumers, who then may spend the money on China-made products, so the "aid" ends up outside the American economy. Counterproductive, anyone?

The Keynesian theory fails because government does not have a vault or a money tree to pluck from. It takes from the people in the form of taxes and loans from domestic and foreign investors, and every dollar it takes from the private sector is a dollar consumers aren't spending. Printing new money simply dilutes the value of money and redistributing what is there is like taking water from one end of a pool and dumping it into the other end—it doesn't raise the water level one bit.

#Keynesian, #Stimulus

Kitchen cabinet

Noun

Refers to the unofficial group of advisers to the president who are usually considered more influential than the official cabinet. The term stems from the story that President Andrew Jackson relied heavily on his unofficial inner circle and met with them in the White House kitchen.

Recent presidents have maintained close ties with the cabinet secretaries of the most weighty departments of state, defense, and the treasury. However, it is uncommon for the president to regularly meet with other department secretaries, and they are usually contacted through his staff. He instead relies heavily on his inner circle of advisers on policy matters and political strategy.

Using a bevy of kitchen cabinet advisers creates a problem, in that it shields the president from congressional oversight. Official cabinet members must be reviewed and confirmed and therefore subject to being checked by Congress. It is much more difficult for the president's staff to be called to testify before a committee due to the ability to exert executive privilege. Kitchen cabinets are an effective place to hide things.

Kleptocracy

Noun

From the Greek *kleptes* ("thief") and *kratos* ("rule"), it is the term used to describe a government run by corrupt leaders who exploit natural resources and embezzle state funds to extend their personal wealth and power. Often there isn't even a pretense of public service.

Typically, kleptocracies are associated with military juntas, dictatorships, and communism. Autocratic and totalitarian regimes are unaccountable to the people and therefore have free reign to use public funds to fill their own personal coffers. Many African nations have historically been controlled by kleptocrats. Oil-rich Equatorial Guinea is one of the most impoverished nations in the world, yet leader Teodoro Obiang Nguema Mbasogo and his family and cohorts live in lavish luxury. U.S. prosecutors in the justice department's Kleptocracy Initiative forced Teodoro's son to give up his $30 million home in Malibu, California, a Ferrari, and Michael Jackson memorabilia. The same effort seized $480 million in assets from the estate of a former Nigerian dictator. These numbers only represent the assets in America and are not representative of the full extent of their corrupt thievery.

Although the United States has made some efforts to curtail kleptocracy in Africa, it is enabling it in Iran. The sanctions relief of $150 billion released to them after the implementation of the nuclear deal, as well as an additional $300–$400 billion from the ability to sell more oil on the open market, will be funneled through the regime and used to continue its oppression of the Iranian people and fund aggressive and terrorist activities.

The same is true of the United States lifting its embargo on the communist nation of Cuba. The people have no private property rights, and there is no independent legislature or legal system to protect them. Every dollar that flows in from opening markets will go directly to the despotic regime that seizes private property and transfers wealth generated by the people to the ruling class. It only strengthens the kleptocratic leaders, thereby furthering the control and poverty of the Cuban people.

Kwanzaa

Holiday

A week-long holiday between December 26 and January 1. The term comes from the Swahili phrase *matunda ya Kwanza*, meaning "first fruits," and is based on African harvest festivals. The official website of Kwanzaa says that the focus is on the seven principles of unity, self-determination, collective work and responsibility, cooperative economics, purpose, creativity, and faith. But collective and cooperative applies only to black people, as it is a celebration devoted to African-American heritage. Kwanzaa is not a religious holiday; it is an *ethnic* holiday.

Although the politically correct media machine glorifies it as a time of unity and reflection, it is important to note the roots of Kwanzaa's founding. Invented in 1966, Kwanzaa was birthed from the mind of Maulana Karenga, founder of the violent black nationalist group, the United Slaves, who was convicted of assault charges in 1971 for torturing two women. He was also at the head of a violent exchange with the Black Panthers on the UCLA campus where two ended up shot dead. Karenga espoused his "seven-fold path of blackness," which was to "think black, talk black, act black, create black, buy black, vote black, and live black."

In a 1978 *Washington Post* article, Karenga was quoted as saying, "People think it's African, but it's not. I came up with Kwanzaa because black people in this country wouldn't celebrate it if they knew it was American. Also, I put it around Christmas because I knew that's when a lot of bloods (blacks) would be partying." Maybe that's why he changed his named to Maulana Karenga. He realized an African "holiday" wouldn't have much credence if founded by a guy named Ronald McKinley Everett.

Author Ann Coulter put the acceptance of it this way,"

It's as if David Duke invented a holiday called "Anglika," which he based on the philosophy of Mein Kampf—and clueless public school teachers began celebrating the made-up, racist holiday.

Kwanzaa is a faux holiday. It's as legitimate as the popular show *Seinfeld*'s "Festivus," in which George Costanza's father made up an alternative to Christmas that included an unadorned aluminum pole and celebrating with a meal and "the airing of grievances" where everyone revealed how they've been disappointed throughout the year and "feats of strength" involving wrestling the head of household. Kwanzaa is a sitcom plot or a punch line; it is not a valid holiday.

Labor union

Plural noun

An organization focused on its members sharing a similar trade or profession put together with the intent of using their size as a means to protect common interests and rights; cultlike organizations intent on their own success, regardless of how it affects the rest of the economy.

Management and labor are both employed by consumers and should naturally function as a team, mutually benefiting one another. However, labor unions drive a wedge between them and make them mortal enemies. They obstruct or remove the most basic principle of *voluntary* exchange: a certain job for a certain wage, allowing both parties to terminate the agreement if the other doesn't adequately meet the terms. Effort, merit, and results should be at the heart of the pact; however, unions ignore all of those elements, focusing instead on their sacrosanct *seniority*.

> *The unions say "last hired, first fired," we say hire and fire based on merit. We want the best and brightest in the classroom.*
>
> —Scott Walker

Unions homogenize workers. They claim to keep wages up by setting minimums but rarely mention that they also set *maximums*. Their directive is that members receive the same wage increase regardless of talent, effort, and skill. An employee cannot negotiate for higher pay, and an employer cannot reward an individual's hard work and initiative—that's not in the contract.

What is in the contract is that the employees *must* join the union and *must* pay dues to this organization that won't allow them to rise above the bar they have set. Members have no say in how the dues are spent—hundreds of millions of dollars of that are funneled into Democratic political campaigns.

Private labor unions are a racket, but public employee unions are even more nefarious. The public-sector employers in charge of budgets and spending of public agencies are also *employees* desiring more income and benefits; therefore, they have no incentive to cut budgets and spending. Public-sector unions have been the foremost cause in driving states into huge debt and bankruptcy. And like their private evil twin, they too contribute millions to political campaigns. The Center for Responsive Politics reports that in 2014 the following contributions were made in the name of unions:

- $26.6 million: National Education Association—100 percent to liberals
- $10.2 million: Carpenters and Joiners Union—95 percent to liberals
- $9.5 million: Democratic Governors Association—100 percent to liberals
- $8.2 million: AFL-CIO—100 percent to liberals
- $4.8 million: American Federation of Government Employees—100 percent to liberals

In gratitude for unions' loyalty, they are awarded grants by federal agencies. Under Obama's tenure the AFL-CIO and SEIU have been given $53 million (taxpayer money), much of which was used to promote and recruit people to sign up for Obamacare (also taxpayer funded). Labor unions do not serve the worker; they serve the Democratic Party. They seek to keep leftist politicians in office to further leftist policies that keep unions in control and their coffers full.

#LaborUnions, #RightToWork

Laissez-faire

Noun

A truly free approach or mentality or policy that involves leaving people to their own devices; a community devoid of government interference and regulations, specifically in the areas of business and economics.

French for "let it go/be," laissez-faire capitalism is a system of thought supporting private ownership and the right to engage in trade of money and goods without arbitrary government restrictions. Some argue that "letting it go" is an unplanned free-for-all allowing for corruption and fraud. That's an erroneous interpretation. Human nature alone dictates that unsavory and fraudulent activities exist in any economic system. Yes, it is the duty of government to protect individuals from fraud and punish those who commit it; however, that has no bearing on the fundamental underpinnings of laissez-faire, which at its core is the informed and *voluntary* exchange that benefits both parties.

Laissez-faire doesn't promote the lack of planning but rather answers the question of *who* should do the planning. The people who are financially and personally invested in the community and success of the business or bureaucrats a thousand miles away seeking to retain power? Laissez-faire certainly does reward businesses with huge profits but only because it also rewards consumers with the products they want. The alternative—government-controlled wages, prices, and availability—rewards greedy bureaucrats with control and power and leaves consumers standing in long lines for the one choice of bread or toilet paper. People do not buy products because government has mandated the company pay a certain wage to its employees or because of EPA regulations or zoning laws. People buy from certain businesses because they like, trust, and can afford their products. If they don't, they go elsewhere. Hence, people across America can choose to type on their MacBooks, Microsoft tablet, or Samsung Galaxy as they sip their almond, soy, or regular milk lattes at Starbucks, Coffee Bean & Tea Leaf, Peet's Coffee, or any of the numerous coffee lounges across the country.

> *Laissez faire does not mean let soulless mechanical forces operate. It means let each individual choose how he wants to cooperate in the social division of labor; let the consumers determine what the entrepreneurs should produce.*
>
> —Ludwig von Mises

Lame duck

Noun

An elected official, such as the president, or group, such as Congress, serving their final term after their successor has been elected. A lame duck session of Congress occurs in even-numbered years when it reconvenes after the November midterm elections. Some members have lost their elections and thus "phone it in" or, conversely, attempt to obstruct legislation. They can become even more obstructive when their party has lost one or both of the chambers.

A lame duck president can be said to have no teeth. He has little time left in office and can lose influence and cooperation with other politicians. On the other hand, knowing his time is almost up, he can take action on unpopular policies or appointments with no fear of consequences.

> *For a member to say, "I'm a lame duck" violates political science 101.*
>
> —Charles Rangel

Democratic New York Representative Charles Rangel is almost never right; however, in the preceding statement he is. Congress is elected to do a job, and they should do so up until their very last moment in office. It is rather laughable, though, Rangel opining about the basics of political service. He has never been a lame duck since he's been in Congress for 127 years—okay, 44—making him part of the permanent political class that only seeks to retain and exploit power, as evidenced by his 11 convicted ethics violations, including housing his political committees in his rent-controlled apartments in Harlem, not paying taxes on his Dominican Republic villa, and not disclosing hundreds of thousands of dollars in assets. Oh for the day he is a lame duck because his existence violates political science 101. And 201. And 301. . . .

Legislative branch

Noun

Article 1, Section 1, of the Constitution states:

> All legislative powers herein granted shall be vested in a Congress of the United States, which shall consist of a Senate and House of Representatives.

The legislative branch is the bicameral body responsible for the origination and passage of bills. According to Section 8, it has the power to borrow money on the credit of the United States, collect taxes, pay debts, and provide for the common defense and general welfare of the United States. It's done a bang-up job borrowing exorbitant amounts of money and collecting taxes. Paying debts . . . not so much. If "providing for the general welfare" means handing out welfare checks to people perfectly capable of working and spending half a billion on a website that didn't work for health insurance that few wanted, then Congress has been successful. But if that's not what it means, then it's clear why the nation is over $17 trillion in debt.

The legislative branch holds the purse strings, and over the past few decades, it has been negligent in cinching them. They pass vague bills (when they actually pass anything) outsourcing policy and spending decisions to regulatory agencies. For example, the

Environmental Protection Agency (EPA) attempts to use the Clean Water Act of 1972 to regulate every puddle and trickle (some on private property) in the name of environmentalism. The National Institutes of Health has a $30 billion budget and claims it would probably find a vaccine for Ebola if not for the lack of funding. They did, however, have enough to spend $387,000 on giving Swedish massages to rabbits. Some other ways in which the legislative branch has not been a good steward of taxpayers' money in 2019:

- $48 billion in 2018 in improper payments to Medicare and Medicaid
- $100,000 to increase the capacity of the Pakistani film industry
- $466,991 grant on studying frog mating calls
- $52 million to do Google Scholar searches, in Hawaii, about the effects of climate hazards
- $150,000 to teach English and information technology skills at Madrassas
- $5.3 million—what NYC agreed to repay on federal funds it accepted to repair junked cars it claimed were damaged by Superstorm Sandy

The legislative branch is the first branch detailed in the Constitution because it is representative of the most important element of the country: the citizens. Its job is to pass bills that protect and support the Constitution and, in the case of disputes, to do nothing at all, because of, well, *gridlock*. This is how it was designed, for maximum liberty for the people. Fewer laws—more freedom.

There is an increasingly pervasive sense not only of failure, but of futility. The legislative process has become a cruel shell game and the service system has become a bureaucratic maze, inefficient, incomprehensible, and inaccessible.

—Elliot Richardson

Liberal

Adjective, noun

A person who subscribes to the views of the Democratic Party. They detest traditional beliefs, believe humans are inherently good and environment is to blame for bad behavior, believe the Constitution is "living" (i.e., malleable), favor special treatment for women and minorities, believe wealth should be redistributed, would prefer religion be believed but not practiced in the public sphere, and believe life should be spearheaded by the government.

Average citizens calling themselves liberals because it's the so-called philosophy of concern, compassion, and freedom have been willingly duped. With this mentality, they are handing over their freedom, their responsibility, and their money to a huge bureaucracy that seeks to control every element of their lives and the lives of everyone else, except sexual behavior and the "right" to kill an unborn baby. Abortion and sex are the only two elements of life that the Left believes individuals have any sort of ability to decide for themselves—ignoring the fact that abortion is a decision to end the life of another.

"Liberal" is a quite a deceptive word. It advocates the freedom of the individual, which classical liberalism once stood for and how the view continues to maintain a positive connotation, but liberal policies remove choice, issue mandates, curb speech, and dictate behavior. Liberals do not birth freedom; they strangle and asphyxiate it.

#LiberalLogic

Liberalism

Noun

A political philosophy founded on the ideas of liberty and equality; often abused in an effort to put the welfare of others into government hands.

Sold as the "compassionate" worldview and champion of the "little guy," liberalism, in fact, sacrifices the little guy at the altar of the supreme state. Liberalism is leftism, which is all government, all the time. Liberalism does not trust individuals to make decisions for themselves, nor does it encourage individuals to take responsibility for the welfare of themselves or those around them. Instead, it insists that the all-knowing government will take care of everything.

Liberals succeed in promoting their views by appealing to feelings rather than logic. It *feels* good to say everyone should make the same amount of money. It *feels* good to push gun control after a mass shooting. It *feels* good to promote health insurance for all. The question they never ask is, "Does it *do* good?"

Liberalism rejects reality. It thrives on those feelings and dreams of utopia. Because the U.S. republic and free-market capitalism are flawed systems, liberals want to destroy it, and as Barack Obama said, "fundamentally transform America." Their solution: a proven *failed* system of the social welfare state. Cradle-to-grave government promises of economic support are unsustainable, as evidenced in the European countries collapsing under the weight of debt incurred by their socialist systems. Despite the failures of Greece, Portugal, Spain, and U.S. states such as California and cities like Detroit that have been under liberal control for decades, liberals refuse to recognize that their philosophy leads to ruin. They continue to push the dream and as a result create a nightmare.

Liberalism is totalitarianism with a human face.

—Thomas Sowell

Libertarian

Noun

A person who believes in individual liberty, personal freedom, free markets, limited government, and nonintervention. At the philosophical heart of libertarianism is the *individual*. Libertarians tend to embrace the mantras of "leave me alone" and "let people do their own thing." They believe individuals should be free to pursue their own lives as long as they respect and do not infringe upon the rights of others.

> *I mean, I've always been a libertarian. Leave everybody alone. Let everybody else do what they want. Just stay out of everybody else's hair.*
>
> —Clint Eastwood

To develop arbitrary laws that prohibit individuals from pursuing happiness in *their own way* is evil incarnate to libertarians. This view comes with a host of problems, though. "Their own way" is a phrase that leaves room for unethical, immoral, and injurious behavior that undermines and threatens society. One's *own way* can be horrifically heinous to a great many. One's *own way* may in fact fly in the face of basic respect for and value of human life. Libertarians often abandon moral positions on "social issues" such as drug legalization, prostitution, same-sex marriage, and abortion. Placing these issues in the category of one's *own way* ignores the moral underpinnings of the nation and has detrimental effects on the individuals themselves and on society as a whole.

The basics of libertarianism are a close cousin of conservatism, and the two are beneficial to one another. Individual liberty, voluntary exchange, minimal government, and strict constitutionality bind them together. Foreign relations and social issues are where they split Libertarians hold a more isolationist point of view and support military action only when the homeland is attacked, tending to believe that foreign endeavors should be relegated to trade and "peaceful diplomacy," which is frankly an unrealistic and dangerous point of view.

Libertarians have a lot to offer conservative efforts and America. The Libertarian Party does not. In fact, it is harmful. Voting for a Libertarian candidate who has no chance of winning hands victory to a Democrat. The majority of principles on which they stand are worthy, but as a political party, libertarianism is feckless and foolish.

#Libertarianism, #Libertarian

Liberty

Noun

Freedom. The fundamental value America was founded upon. (See **Freedom**.) Liberty is the lifeblood of the nation and only possible with a limited government. The more the state controls, the less liberty a citizen has.

> *We hold these truths to be self-evident: that all men are created equal; that they are endowed by their Creator with certain unalienable rights; that among these are life, liberty, and the pursuit of happiness.*
>
> —Thomas Jefferson

Liberty is a God-given right that allows for the pursuit of happiness. Government is meant to protect it, not destroy it.

#Liberty, #SweetLandOfLiberty, #Freedom

Lobby

Verb, noun

To lobby is to advocate for and influence government policy. It is protected under the First Amendment with "the right of the people peaceably to assemble, and to petition the government for a redress of grievances." Lobbyists present information and analysis of special interests and offer assessment on the effects of bills.

The term has its roots in the mid-17th century when citizens would assemble in a lobby near the English House of Commons to state their views to Members of Parliament. Now lobbying is not simply a gathering of average citizens seeking the ear of politicians but a multi-billion-dollar business greatly influencing policy. It is a right and it is valuable, but it also corrupt. Not all efforts, of course, but some. And it is simply the nature of the beast of humanity. Some members of the legislature bow to special interests in order to maintain their position or fatten their wallets. There's no doubt that lobbying has tainted the political process, but it is beneficial as well. It allows for otherwise silent citizens to voice their opinions via contributions to a group that supports their views. Lobbyist organizations have access to congresspeople that the average Joe does not; therefore, it is a vital tool in petitioning representatives.

Lubrication

Noun

One of the newest additions to the vernacular of second-grade students in government schools, coming from the incredible new sex-ed curriculum. Here's a sample of some of the new directives:

- "Wetter Makes It Better"
- "Got Lube?"
- "Forget to Pick Up the Lube? Use Plenty of Saliva"

Machine politics

Noun

Specific to U.S. politics, a large political group with an autocratic leader who attains enough power to maintain charge in a region. The machine retains its power by corralling the poor and doling out benefits to keep them compliant, reliant, and loyal. It also engages in quid pro quos with business and labor leaders demanding and rewarding actions that benefit the party.

Nineteenth-century New York City was the epitome of machine politics under Democratic Tammany Hall, the organization that ran the city and birthed what became known as the spoils system. The leaders threw their support behind presidential candidate Andrew Jackson, and when elected, he rewarded them with federal jobs, simultaneously purging those in opposition to his policies. Tammany functioned like a political mafia: employing threats, payoffs, and bribery to maintain its stronghold on the city.

Today, the city of Chicago, where Barack Obama began his political career, carries on the tradition of Tammany Hall. It's no wonder his administration engaged in the underhanded tactics of the IRS targeting of conservative groups, spying on and intimidating journalists and a presidential candidate, and handing billions of dollars to failing companies and rogue foreign regimes. Machine politics is about flexing government muscle. Oppose the ruling class and it will coldcock you and knock you out.

> *The political machine triumphs because it is a united minority acting against a divided majority.*
>
> —Will Durant

#PoliticalMachine, #MachinePolitics, #Tammany

MAGA

Acronym for a movement

MAGA is the acronym for "Make America Great Again," the 2016 Donald J. Trump for president slogan. Embraced by patriots nationwide, it served to affirm that America is the land of the free and home of the brave. Trump then had the audacity to project MAGA on the world stage, revamping old trade deals and asserting a new fairness doctrine, while representing those core values and the opportunities they offer to the world. After all, America has, in the recent two centuries, accomplished the greatest leap in prosperity known to mankind—for the entire world. And it's because of capitalism, which harnesses the inherent self-preservation tendencies of man (the individual sovereign) together with the free market to inspire creativity and problem solving and then offers those solutions to the largest possible consumer base.

Gee, amazing that the first successful, true capitalist elected president in a long time would promote that most fair and equitable of economic systems and proceed to win over the world (except for the devout leftists.)

#MAGA, #Trump, #AmericaFirst, #AmericaStrong

Mainstream media or MSM

Noun

The infotainment conglomerate. Also known as "lapdog media" and "lamestream media." Unindicted co-conspirators.

Because power corrupts and information is power, the media gradually self-corrupted. Now it seeks to manipulate, influence, and distract by pretending to inform. Most of the mainstream news sources, NBC, ABC, CBS, CNN, MSNBC, CNBC, and so on, are owned by only a very few media corporations that also own most of the large corporate entertainment industry. Strangely, many of the higher, profile players are related to politicians. This is a conflict for the average Joe Plumber because the Fourth Estate (the media) is intended to hold politicians accountable. Well, that stopped when they got married. Now we only have talk radio and some upstarts, OAN, America's Voice, and NewsMax, who refuse to carry water for the politicians who are drunk on their own power.

This was the power structure during Obama's tenure in office:

- ABC News executive producer Ian Cameron—**husband** to Susan Rice, national security adviser
- CBS President David Rhodes—**brother** of Ben Rhodes, Obama's deputy national security adviser for strategic communications
- ABC News correspondent Claire Shipman—**wife** of White House press secretary Jay Carney
- ABC News and Univision reporter Matthew Jaffe—**husband** to Obama's deputy press secretary Katie Hogan
- ABC President Ben Sherwood—**brother** of Obama's special adviser Elizabeth Sherwood
- CNN President Virginia Moseley—**wife** of Hillary Clinton's former deputy secretary Tom Nides
- Clinton's White House communications director, George Stephanopolous, became a "journalist" at ABC after leaving the White House because he was so good at making up stuff.

The associations are innumerable. Now, if you believe that all politicians are alike and that Trump has a similar bench of enamored reporters, just check his coronavirus briefings or almost any article in virtually any publication. Facebook, Google, and YouTube are arrayed against him as well. There's also this: five major corporations control roughly 90 percent of our media. Guess which way they tilt?

- NBC Comcast: NBC, MSNBC, CNBC, Telemundo, Sky, E!, Universal Pictures, BuzzFeed, Focus Features
- Disney: ABC, ESPN, Pixar, Miramax, Marvel Studios, History Channel, Nat Geo, Hulu, 21st Century Fox, Fox Entertainment
- Viacom-CBS: CBS News, CBS Entertainment Group, MTV, Nick Jr, BET, CMT, Paramount Pictures, Simon and Schuster, Showtime, Smithsonian Channel, NFL.com, Jeopardy, *60 Minutes*
- ATT-Warner Bros: CNN, HBO, Cinemax, TMZ, Time, Warner Bros., Cartoon Network, Warner Music Group, Hachette Livre, Turner, DC Comics, TBS, TNT
- NewsCorp: Fox News, *New York Post*, *Wall Street Journal*, HarperCollins

Notice anything odd? The smallest one of the five major info-tainment distributors skews more neutral than the rest. None of them are conservative—out of all sources! Take a look at this illustration: https://fortune.com/longform/media-company-ownership-consolidation/.

It's like a word cloud from a rabid social justice warrior meet-up. None of the major conservative outlets, Breitbart, *Washington Post*, or CBN, to name a few, appear because they are so small in comparison.

> *He who controls the medium controls the message. He who controls the message controls the masses.*
>
> —Joseph Goebbels

Malthus, Reverend Thomas (1776–1834)

Person

An English cleric and scholar, author of *An Essay on the Principle of a Population*, who believed that population growth inhibits progress toward a utopia. His basic premise was that birth rate would outpace the food supply leading to catastrophic events such as famine and war. The Malthusian theory seemed plausible at the time, given that food production increased at a much slower pace than population, but with the advent of technology and increased agricultural production and trade, that misguided theory quickly lost its luster.

Although his hypothesis was incorrect, Malthus did make a salient point in later editions of his essay regarding social problems arising out of depravity. He emphasized using moral restraint to curb an increase in lower-class poverty. The lack of self-control and foresight of consequences could lead to untenable circumstances. Sadly, his proposed solution flew in the face of liberty, because he argued for forced sterilization and criminalization for people who had more children than they could afford. Presumably, he himself or some random appointed bureaucrats would sit in judgment over everyone.

Mandate

Noun

An official order, condition, requirement, or restriction issued from the government with forced compliance. There are mandates at local levels—cities banning plastic bags and requiring that businesses charge for paper ones, for instance. At the state level, California issued directives mandating a raise of the minimum wage, paid sick leave, and a forced reduction of water usage by up to 35 percent.

Initially, the nation's COVID-19 response efforts intended to reduce the curve—to protect from a surge of cases that might overwhelm our healthcare system. But when that falsely predicted surge failed to materialize, disappointed Democrats, drunk on the additional power bestowed to them by general panic and fear, saw a great crisis to exploit to strengthen their stranglehold. Recently, many liberal governors have mandated wearing masks to slow the spread of COVID-19. One ought to ask why. Why forestall the inevitable? One should also ask to see proof that mask wearing does indeed produce the desired results. One would then learn that they don't exist.

A CDC report from 2010 indicates that cloth masks "may provide marginal protection against nanoparticles," but the illusion of safety is more compelling than truth, so masks are mandated.

One doesn't ask. One only submits and obeys in our new COVID-19 society.

Federal mandates are especially egregious via its *unelected* agencies: on the environment, health, education, labor . . . well, all of them, really.

The most important quality of a mandate is its unreasonableness. For instance, D.C. Mayor Muriel Bowser's mask mandate ordered three-year-olds to cover their faces but excepted lawmakers and government employees while "on duty."

Don't ask why—just comply. Got it?

A mandate only illustrates an authoritarian, elitist mentality: *I know better than you idiots. Period.*

Mask hysteria

Noun

A term coined by yours truly Sam Sorbo to describe the religious fervor for the belief that masks will stop the spread of the coronavirus. Also the mania that results from oxygen deprivation and excess CO_2 due to wearing a mask.

This should not be confused with "mass kiss-teria"!

According to a CDC study from June of 2010, "the use of fabric materials may provide only minimal levels of respiratory protection to a wearer against virus-size submicron aerosol particles." There exist no study to effectively argue for wearing masks and many demonstrations showing the hazards of wearing them (all of which seem to violate social media mogul guidelines and have been removed), and yet folks are still touting the "wear your mask" slogans and assaulting people outdoors, even, for not participating in face diapering and voice dampening. They are losing their minds about muzzles, especially where it concerns others. Have you heard of anything so ridiculous as "Wear your mask for others, and they wear theirs for you"? (See also **Face diaper**.)

McCarthyism

Noun

Webster's defines McCarthyism as "the practice of making accusations of disloyalty, especially of pro-Communist activity, in many instances unsupported by proof or based on slight, doubtful, or irrelevant evidence."

Well, when put like that, who wouldn't hate Joe McCarthy? Small problem: those accusations are entirely *false*. McCarthy suffers the equivalent of a fisherman's recounting of his day on the boat—by the end of his story-telling rounds, the six-inch trout had evolved into a 20-foot great white shark.

Losers marching in leftist lockstep launch the lingo whenever someone questions their lies or corruption or presents an opposition to their claims. They weep for the poor communist Hollywood writers questioned by Joe McCarthy, who they assert was a hammer in search of a nail, on a smear campaign devoid of evidence. But the truth is that communism was (and still is) a very real and present danger (including, now, in our schools). Not only had Soviet spies infiltrated the deepest levels of government, threatening national security, but naive or complicit officials ignored, lied about, and covered up the penetration. Senator Joe McCarthy sought to uncover and root out the threat. He was a national hero who did the nation a great service.

Means testing

Noun

An examination of a person's or family's income to determine eligibility for government financial assistance. Used in Chapter 7 bankruptcy, welfare programs, Medicare Part B premiums, it has been suggested for all of Medicare and Social Security.

The United States spends over $900 billion a year on means-tested welfare programs for food, cash, housing, medical care, social services, and training. Since the War on Poverty began in the 1960s, we've spent more than $22 trillion, and for the past 20 years, it has been the government's fastest-growing expenditure.

There is no longer any requirement to seek employment, education, or training as part of the deal. Means testing is based on supposed need only. There is no incentive to work, and there are no consequences to remaining willfully unemployed. The problem is, people will continue to "need" it as long as the government feeds (and funds) the need.

#Welfare, #WelfareState

Mercantilism

Noun

An economic theory in which a country exports more goods than it imports. This was the main economic system in 16th- to 18th-century nations, resting on the idea that the only way to prosperity was to hoard precious metals (gold and silver) and place high tariffs on imported goods. It was unsustainable. Erecting high tariffs and trade barriers encouraged other nations to do the same, creating a never-ending game of escalation that ultimately strangled international trade.

Scottish philosopher Adam Smith dismantled the paradigm of a mercantilist system in his 1776 treatise, *The Wealth of Nations*, by using the example of winemaking. Scotland could only grow worthwhile grapes in hothouses, which would cost exorbitant amounts of money to heat, thereby making Scottish wines 30 times more expensive than French wines. But Scotland had a lot more sheep than France, and he reasoned that trading wool for wine would benefit both the consumers of France and Scotland. Nations have different natural resources and production abilities, so it was far more profitable for both producers and consumers to trade what they readily have for less accessible goods.

But mercantilism isn't concerned with the consumer; it's concerned with control. Its purpose: to build a powerful state by colluding with the commercial class forcing regulation, inhibiting others from entering the field, and imposing tariffs and quotas on competing manufactured imports. Mercantilism is a *managed* economy in which the prices are fixed not by demand but by the government.

Note: The "trade war" that Trump is managing with China is an outgrowth of the understanding that China is not dealing fairly with the United States, its trade *partner*. By currency manipulation and outright subterfuge and theft, China is taking advantage of America's generous spirit, and that needs to stop. Instigating "leveling tariffs" is not the same as mercantilism.

'Merica

Noun

Let's just say that the Robertson dynasty inspired this shortening of America to its grass-roots, home-grown, duck-calling best. It represents all we love about this great country: freedom, faith, and family. Also, it evokes a down-home, relaxed vibe we can all appreciate. America is a family of people who want the autonomy to sink or swim individually. We are proud of our predecessors' accomplishments—advancements shared around the world. This nation is great not because we dominate by force but because we lead by example.

Microaggression

Noun

The newest term the Left has invented to claim victimhood status where none is deserved. For instance, a UCLA professor corrected a student's paper to reflect the *Chicago Manual of Style* (as required in the class) by changing his capitalized word "indigenous" to lowercase. The professor was accused of a microaggression for failing to honor the student's attempt to highlight the (perceived) importance of being indigenous.

Claiming microaggressions—things too small to perceive but just big enough to imagine—is a power grab by the Left. The professor's job is to teach, but he was reprimanded for doing his job. Conforming to the current zeitgeist of feelings-over-facts is a betrayal of goodness, truth, and beauty and a descent into lunacy because then nothing is real but one's own imaginings.

> *To accuse people of aggression for not marching in lockstep with political correctness is to set the stage for justifying real aggression against them.*
>
> —Thomas Sowell

Microtyranny

Noun

Perhaps originally coined by Thomas Sowell in an article about microaggression. A term popularized by Charlie Kirk, microtyranny develops when seemingly powerless people find opportunity in correcting or dictating to others. For instance, with mask hysteria, many people eagerly embrace the chance to virtue signal by insisting others follow the arbitrary and freedom-stifling new rules.

Military

Noun, adjective

The organization of armed forces. In the United States, the purpose of the military is to protect and defend the freedoms illuminated in the Declaration of Independence and Constitution. It is a necessary force to fight against foreign elements that seek to destroy liberty.

A military is a well-organized, disciplined, and focused fighting machine. Some nations use their militaries to conquer people and territories and enforce a despotic rule. America's military must always seek to be superior because it seeks only to protect and serve, and other, tyrannical forces seek only to advance. The evil of tyranny must be crushed. It is America's military might that has defeated and protected the free world from the threats of fascism, communism, and Islamism. A strong and feared American military creates a safer world for all peoples.

> *I look forward to a great future for America—a future in which our country will match its military strength with our moral restraint, its wealth with our wisdom, its power with our purpose.*
>
> —John F. Kennedy

#Military, #Army, #Navy, #AirForce, #USMC, #StrongMilitary

Militia

Noun

Ordinary citizens supplied with some training and their own weapons organized to fight and defend in emergencies, invasions, or overreaching government.

The Second Amendment states, "A well regulated militia, being necessary to the security of a free state, the right of the people to keep and bear arms, shall not be infringed." Similarly, Thomas Jefferson wrote "For a people who are free, and who mean to remain so, a well-organized and armed militia is their best security." Our Founders' experience with British rule and knowledge of its history gave them a tremendous mistrust of a national standing army. Britain often used its own army to oppress its citizens. The militia called upon citizens to collectively organize and assume arms to defend themselves and their community or state against violence.

But militias went the way of the dodo fairly quickly as the military forces of the United States became centralized and federalized.

> *I ask, sir, what is the militia? It is the whole people except for a few public officials.*
>
> —George Mason

Minimum wage

Noun

First introduced nationally in 1938, minimum wage is the lowest amount of financial pay an employer must give a worker. But truthfully, the actual minimum wage is zero—because if the work doesn't merit the government-enforced, artificially high pay, there's no job.

Initial minimum wage laws wreaked havoc on the black community, typically the lowest-paid workers. Currently, the fight for raising the minimum wage rests on wages being too low to raise a family on. But the intention of minimum-wage jobs was always entry-level positions for folks new to the workforce, to give them work experience and entice employers to take a chance on someone with little-to-no skills. If the government artificially raises the pay level, then the employer must hire only those whose work aptitude rises to that level, and that disenfranchises the young and the inexperienced out of entry-level positions, virtually crippling them from ever working productively.

Minimum-wage hikes always sound great to unthinking voters, but they instigate a rise in prices, typically hitting minimum-wage earners the hardest. It may be an attractive political ploy, but for the savvy voter, it's just pandering.

The second, equally important argument against raising minimum wages is that it's a hidden tax hike. With any wage paid, an employer pays a percentage in taxes, as does the employee. Higher wages—higher tax revenues. Kinda makes ya think, huh?

*Making it illegal to pay less than a given amount does not make
a worker's productivity worth that amount—and, if it is not,
that worker is unlikely to be employed.*

—Thomas Sowell, author of *Basic Economics:
A Citizen's Guide to the Economy*

Misogynist

Noun

Originally meaning someone who hates women, the term is now
diluted to mean *man*. This generalization occurred as feminists
insisted that men demeaned women by seeing them as sex partners.
Of course, it's ridiculous, because men's sexuality is such that they
objectify objects of their desire. It's kinda written into the word itself.
But because feminists are determined to strip women of any femi-
ninity, they equally seek to eradicate men. Which is funny, because
how does the Left define man in the age of self-determination? The
good news is that you can totally decide for yourself which gender
you are (of the 74 existing ones—but at this point, who's counting?).
Hint: Don't choose man, because there's a war against them in the
culture.

*You have to go to college to think that men who see women they
find attractive as sex objects hate women.*

—Dennis Prager

Monopoly

Noun

Ownership of the entire market for a specific good or service.

In the eponymous board game, when the racecar player lands
on Boardwalk and buys it and then lands on Park Place and buys
it, he gets to charge double the rent. Why? Because those are the

fanciest properties on the board. However, the racecar's ownership of Boardwalk and Park Place doesn't restrict others from competing in the real estate market. It is not prohibitive or destructive to the economy because the iron player can still purchase Pacific Avenue and the other upscale green properties, where he can then build houses and hotels.

In a free-market capitalistic system, the only way a business can oust its competition is to provide better products at a lower cost. If a monopoly results, so be it. The company *earned* it with good business practices. A natural monopoly such as this, however, is usually short lived because there is always a threat of competition by another ambitious, dedicated entrepreneur who will rise up and challenge it.

The attack on private-enterprise monopolies as evil is a myth used to further the call for government intervention in private business. In reality, it is government's manipulation and control that create monopolies. When the government institutes any law prohibiting others from entering an industry or regulations restricting access to an industry, that is how the true evil arises.

> *Our public school system is our country's biggest and most inefficient monopoly, yet it keeps demanding more and more money.*
>
> —Phyllis Schlafly

Mostly peaceful

Noun

In a report on CNN's *Early Start* show on August 25, 2020, the chyron read, "FIERY BUT MOSTLY PEACEFUL PROTESTS AFTER POLICE SHOOTING," over a shot of a building and cars engulfed in a raging fire. CNN was soundly mocked for this incredible attempt to destigmatize outright violence. Make no mistake—some kinds of violence are perfectly justifiable to leftists. Jonathan Turley cleverly detected that CNN critically failed to include the words "looty," "assault," and "shooty." Radio show host Chris Plante immediately adopted mostly peaceful as a catch phrase—noting that CNN never qualified the *actually peaceful* Trump rallies with such apologies. CNN's mental gymnastics are worse than, "Other than that, Mrs. Lincoln, how did you enjoy the play?"

Muckraker

Noun

A journalist focused on investigative reporting to expose the scandal, corruption, and underbelly of powerful institutions of business and government. The term found fame after a 1906 Teddy Roosevelt speech where he referenced John Bunyan's *The Pilgrim's Progress*: "the man with the muck-rake, the man who could look no way but downward."

Although Roosevelt was supportive of them, he cautioned,

> The man who never does anything else, who never thinks
> or speaks or writes, save of his feats with the muck-rake,
> speedily becomes, not a help to society, not an incitement to
> good, but one of the most potent forces for evil.

The crusade for truth can be defiled when a reporter has reached a conclusion before he or she has uncovered the evidence. Wading in and searching through only muck can blind one to reality and consequently entice one to "muck up" the truth to suit an agenda. When that occurs, muckraking becomes "yellow journalism," where sensationalizing, attacking, ridiculing, and defaming supersedes facts. For examples of yellow journalism, tune in to MSNBC or CNN, where it seems to run on a continuous loop.

National debt

Noun

Although the national debt is grammatically a noun, it certainly seems more like a verb because it is continuously climbing! Having just jumped above $19 trillion, the spending of the federal government seems completely detached from any budget. The national debt is the accumulation of *all* yearly deficits in the history of the country. Under Clinton, the *national debt* grew by 36 percent. For Bush, the cumulative debt also grew by that much. In two terms, President Obama more than doubled the national debt during the slowest economic recovery in history, ballooning it by 84 percent. Time will tell how it fares under Trump, who managed the most incredible return to productivity and economic growth, only to be derailed by COVID-19.

NAZI

Noun

Acronym for the party of the National Socialist German Workers' Party, led by Adolf Hitler, and major perpetrator of genocidal atrocities in World War II. Included here because leftists successfully have redefined the Nazis as being synonymous with "right wing." As if there were "right wing" socialists and then the other kind—just socialists—who are oh-so-wonderful. The fact is that after World War II, the communists and socialists didn't want to be affiliated with these National Socialists who had just been punished on the world stage for their atrocities. So communists and socialists started a campaign to make the *nationalism* part of the party name the bad part. The *socialism* aspect of what the Nazis did, with enforcing groupthink, government takeovers, and militarization, was completely forgotten! Suddenly, it's simply that the Germans *loved* their country too much, and that was *bad*. Obviously, it's ridiculous. Mainly because what the Nazis did was not different from what the communists did, and in fact, the Nazis cooperated with the communists for as long as it served them to obtain power.

The sad thing is that Stalin, a communists and one of the world's worst murderers, sat in judgment over the Nazi war criminals. That was perhaps the greatest hypocrisy accepted by the world.

> *America is like a healthy body and its resistance threefold: its patriotism, its morality and its spiritual life. If we can undermine these three areas, America will collapse from within.*
>
> —Joseph Stalin

Newsheimers

Noun

The name we use for when media forgets a story they covered because it currently contradicts the new narrative or because they are pushing a new story that hurts the president. But I repeat myself. Radio show host Chris Plante originated it and uses is often, sadly.

The easy forgetfulness is a product of the Communist Party, where the truth is simply what the current party directors espouse. That's why, when Stalin killed Trotsky, suddenly all the Trotskyites disavowed any affection for their late "dear" leader.

Nomination

Noun

The act of proposing a person for a candidacy or appointment to office. Prior to a party's presidential nomination, candidates campaign with a focus on reaching their party's voters. After a long season of vying for the position, state delegates vote, and then an official announcement of the nomination is made at the Democrat and Republican National Conventions.

Once in office, leaders may make nominations for agency and judicial positions, for consideration by the bodies charged with acting on those nominations.

#GOPConvention, #DNCConvention

NPC or monplayer character

Noun

The nonplayer characters in video games are characters inserted by the developer to interact with players but only in limited capacity. They are not thinking. They have few limited responses like, "Do not give in to the power of the Legion." They are like social media "bots"—short for robots—that perform a function but never reach beyond their designed purpose.

NPC is a term now used to label someone who subscribes so strongly to an ideology that they stop thinking for themselves and allow that ideology to define them and determine their actions. Sadly, our education has adeptly trained children to behave in this fashion, so it seems that more and more people choose not to think independently but would rather just play follow the leader.

Obamacare (Affordable Healthcare Act)

Noun

An abomination, in so much as it was predicated on lies and tyranny. A socialism-lovers' form of "healthcare" *forced* upon the American people (by mandate) and enforced as a tax while allowing those who wrote it to be exempted. The Affordable Care Act is over 2,000 pages long. Nancy Pelosi stupidly crooned, "We have to pass the bill so that you can find out what is in it." Those who voted for it had not even read it.

The president promoted it as a way for everyone to get health insurance while lowering costs. How that might be possible by sending all the insurance money from the open markets through a government bureaucracy he never explained. He dismissed concerns about being forced onto new plans or having to change doctors with his repeated rhetoric: "If you like your health plan, you can keep your health plan. If you like your doctor, you can keep your doctor. Period." Both now proven lies. He also promised a $2,500 savings to each family. (Still waiting!)

- Millions were kicked off their plans because they did not meet the Obamacare "standards."
- The Congressional Budget Office (CBO) estimates that 31 million people will still be uninsured in the next 10 years.
- The Government Accountability Office (GAO) reported that $840 billion was spent on the Healthcare.gov website because it didn't work. Initial work on the failed website was performed in Canada.
- Many of the people who enrolled in the exchanges made just a little too much to qualify for subsidies and now pay

more than they did prior to enactment or they opted to go without insurance and pay the penalty.

- The second cheapest plan, the "Silver Plan," premiums have gone up on average 7.5 percent from 2015 to 2016, 36 percent in Oklahoma and 34 percent in Montana.

Incidentally, Pelosi was right about one thing: "After we pass this bill, being a woman will no longer be a preexisting medical condition."

The Affordable Care Act is not affordable, and Obama doesn't care.

#ObamaCare, #ACA, #ObamCareFail

Obamunism

Noun

The term Ken Matthews used for the eight years of specialist ideology President Obama injected into the American political and economic system. Obama famously claimed he was going to "fundamentally transform" us into this amalgamation of horrors, and he went a long way, from overburdensome regulations of industry to the eponymous Obamacare. But America has won a reprieve, and a soft rescue is what the Trump presidency offers. Unfortunately, a great deal of the damage has already been done in simply the way our youth thinks (or fails to think).

Critical race theory is being forced into our children's schools. It's being imposed into workplace trainings, and it's being deployed to rip apart friends, neighbors, and families.

Oligarchy

Noun

A government where the power is concentrated in the hands of a few people. It is maintained through royalty, wealth, corporate dominance, or military or religious control and is often transferred through family lines.

Some label the United States an oligarchy. When compared to a theoretical ideal of a utopian democracy, then yes, the United States falls short. And yes, corporations and the wealthy do have more influence than they probably should in our political system; however, when compared to the true authoritarian oligarchs of China, Russia, and even European nations (controlled by the European Union), where there is faint chance of the little guy having any influence, the United States stands head and shoulders above the rest of the world for the democratic process.

A leadership class in a system does not define it as an oligarchy. The idea that *everyone* could possibly have the same input and participation is unrealistic. Even primitive packs of animals have a pecking order. Without leadership, there is no organization.

Parliamentary government

Noun

A system in which the executive is chosen by the legislature. The public votes for representatives in parliament (the equivalent of the U.S. Congress), and the dominant party then appoints its leader as prime minister. The United States distinguishes itself from this system in one very important way: separation of powers. In the United States, the president is elected separately from the legislature, can be of a different party from Congress, and can veto legislation that crosses his or her desk. In a parliamentary government, the executive (prime minister) *is* the legislature.

Parliamentary governments vary from country to country in procedure and elections. Their commonality is that the passage of policy is consolidated in the legislature alone. Many also lack a written constitution outlining their duties, and as a result, governing laws can fluctuate depending upon who's in power. No set election dates allow for a prime minister to call an election at his or her will, and a vote of no confidence can be taken to oust him or her, which leaves the prime minister vulnerable to the winds of popular opinion. Although there is typically less gridlock in a parliamentary system, it leaves little room for opposition to effectively challenge the party in power.

We can't afford to go down the dead end roads of Parliamentary Socialism or Fascistic Bolshevism.

—John Blair (Founding Father and renowned jurist)

Party-line voting

Verb

Casting a vote in tune with a political party, regardless of reason, facts, conscience, or the views of the voters' constituents.

The majority of Democrats in Congress *toed the party line* when they voted for the Iran nuclear deal. They ignored irrefutable facts, dismissed the dangers, caved to the peer pressure of their party, and joined in the smoking of the crack pipe that currently still threatens the safety and security of the United States, Israel, and much of the world.

Party-line voting is a sign of weak-willed, power-hungry political animals that seek recognition, favor, and permanent standing in their party's establishment.

> *The House of Representatives was not designed to sit idly by and rubberstamp every piece of legislation sent their way by the Senate, especially legislation passed on a straight party line vote under the spurious policy of reconciliation.*
>
> —Neal Boortz (attorney and talk show host)

#Lockstep, #Establishment

Patriotic

Adjective

Vigorous, loyal supporters of the nation. To be patriotic is to be proud of, love, and defend the symbols, beliefs, and principles of one's county. Having national pride.

In 2008, just prior to his election, President Obama stated, "We are five days away from fundamentally transforming America." Patriots honor and love their country. If one loves something, one may want to improve it—after all, nothing is perfect. But to *fundamentally transform* it? Radio talk-show host Dennis Prager has pointed out that if a woman said she wanted to fundamentally transform her husband on their wedding day, it wouldn't be plausible to believe that she really loves him. As a wife respects, values, and honors what her husband stands for, so a patriot does for his or her country. In his quote, Obama showed tremendous disdain for the country, and his actions bear out that conclusion.

> *A man's country is not a certain area of land, of mountains, rivers, and woods, but it is a principle; and patriotism is loyalty to that principle.*
>
> —George William Curtis (American writer and speaker)

Peace Force

Noun

Proposed by Denver City Councilwoman Candi CdeBaca in the wake of the George Floyd incident and resulting civil unrest, the Peace Force is meant to abolish and replace the Denver Police Department, which CdeBaca claims disproportionately polices communities of color. She also believes that violence results from job or food insecurity, transience, and homelessness, as opposed to the more time-tested factors of anger and the lack of morals and self-control.

The Left seeks chaos. Police traditionally stand for order. What better way to achieve destruction than to foment distrust, hatred, and anger and remove the element of control. But let's face it, without morality—self-government and self-restraint—this nation and its freedoms cannot stand. No amount of laws or police can maintain peace without the will of the governed or, in absence of that, guns and tyranny (which is what the Left wants).

Philosopher

Noun

A person who seeks knowledge, wisdom, and enlightenment by attempting to think out the best way to be and live. A philosopher's best endeavor is the pursuit of clarity with virtue.

Aristotle dedicated much of his thought to the nature of virtues in his writing of *Ethics*. He used logic, reason, and observable facts to apply order in a disordered world, to dissect the importance of what is right and good versus our selfish desires to obtain what is easy, comfortable, or powerful. His philosophy is completely at odds with the prevalent subjective thinking of today—that good is whatever we say it is, whatever we want it to be.

Respectable philosophers know their duty is to discover truth, not to create it.

#Philosophers, #Aristotle, #Ethics

Pithy

Adjective

Meaning short and sweet, top-rated TV personality Bill O'Reilly branded this term on his immensely popular news commentary show *The O'Reilly Factor*.

Pizzagate

Noun

Refers to a theory that a Washington, DC, pizza restaurant served (or still serves) as a hub for child sex trafficking involving many of the elite and powerful businesspeople, politicians, and celebrities.

The email of Hillary Clinton's chief of staff, John Podesta, was allegedly hacked and discovered to contain some very strange language that served as the Pizzagate narrative. According to legend, certain food items, some of which appear in the emails, represent types of children-on-order. "Cheese pizza" means child pornography, for instance. And there are the people who have died—suicides, even—surrounding these odd things.

Take Jeffrey Epstein, the world's most notorious pedophile, for an example, but don't forget that authorities at his maximum security facility took him off suicide watch, put him in a room by himself, and allowed his monitoring cameras to malfunction. Then his guards fell asleep, and he strangled himself impossibly with a bedsheet— not by hanging. Now add a little of *nobody* saying *anything* about his predilections—not even a "Wow, I had no idea any of that was happening on his private island"—despite being on his plane multiple times. After that, throw in the massive amounts of media devoted to debunking and dispelling all those crazy rumors as totally ridiculous far-right-wing conspiracy theories, and you understandably get a little suspicious.

Nothin' to see here, folks. It's not like pedophiles actually exist. It's not like the North American Man/Boy Love Association actually has a website and advocates for men to join the Boy Scouts because it provides fertile hunting territory for vulnerable young boys. It's not like Chrissy Teigen has posted explicitly pedophiliac musings ("seeing little girls do the splits half naked is just . . . i [sic] want to put myself in jail") or Twitter changed its rules to accommodate pedophiles, too.

Wait, though. That stuff is all real. . . .

#Pizzagate, #Pedogate, #Qanon

Plandemic

Noun

The name of a documentary that postulates that the COVID-19 pandemic was a scheduled, nefariously intended attack on our society by a cabal that wants to force vaccinations. Roundly panned by many mainstream outlets as a kooky collection of conspiracy-theory falsehoods, the video nonetheless offers some compelling evidence, like the recorded warnings of a coming pandemic by many of the people involved in the origins of the virus who are now running the response. The prohibition by many of the media platforms and general derision and discrediting helped fuel interest in the video, which garnered millions of hits.

Whatever you do, don't watch this movie!

The lady doth protest too much, methinks.

—*Hamlet*, Act III, Scene II, 210–219

Planned Parenthood

Nonprofit organization

Planned Parenthood is the number one abortion provider in America. They also claim to provide reproductive maternal and child health services. They are proud contributors to the eight million plus African-American abortions completed in the last 20 years. Performing over 300,000 abortions per year and classified as a nonpartisan, nonprofit provider of women's "preventative healthcare," Planned Parenthood also donates millions to the Democratic Party, a party that claims to stand for women's rights—just not the rights of unborn or preborn women, or even postborn women. In 2019, several Democrats supported legislation securing an adult's option to terminate a pregnancy after the child was born. Liberals and the mainstream media carry the toxic water of this organization, claiming it provides invaluable services for women that are otherwise unavailable, ignoring *the other 9,000 free clinics that operate nationwide.*

Defending the half a billion dollars of federal funding per year, U.S. Secretary of Health and Human Services Sylvia Mathews Burwell said, "What I think is important is that our HHS funding is focused on issues of preventative care for women, things like mammograms."

Except Planned Parenthood doesn't offer mammograms; it offers mammogram referrals.

After the 2015 release of a series of videos revealing Planned Parenthood's harvesting and selling of baby body parts for profit, columnist Michelle Malkin accurately summarized their barbarism with

> The exposé comes after years of undercover journalistic work by Lila Grace Rose and Live Action, who have caught government-supported Planned Parenthood officials covering up for sexual predators, promoting gendercide, flouting health regulations and disclosure laws, soliciting money from racist eugenics zealots who want more black babies aborted, and perpetuating a homicidal racket in the name of "reproductive health."

Planned Parenthood does not *plan parenthood*; it obliterates it. It is not a women's preventive healthcare organization; it is baby butcher shop.

#DefundPP, #AbortionHorrors, #PPact

Platform (political)

Noun

The fundamental principles, policies, and goals to which a political party adheres. With each presidential cycle, the Republican and Democratic committees write and release a comprehensive document outlining and explaining its party's current views and objectives.

In 2012, the Republican platform selected the slogan, "We Believe in America," while the Democratic platform chose, "Moving America Forward." The phrases may sound gimmicky, but they reveal truth about each party's ideology. Republicans abide by the tenets of the nation's founding: the Constitution, small government, virtue, liberty, and the vital importance of the traditional family.

Democrats, on the other hand, used "moving forward" as a smokescreen to hide their innate disapproval of those same principles. They employ "forward" to convince the public of their intended good. But forward is only detrimental if the march moves in the wrong direction. Would it be wise to move forward along a trail of fire toward a gas station?

Platforms encompass many details about a wide array of policies but define the broader view of the role of government. As they say, look behind the curtain.

> *The Republican platform specifically says we don't believe in bailing out private business, and yet we did.*
>
> —Rand Paul

#GOPPlatform, #DemocratPlatform, #RNC, #DNC

Plutocracy

Noun

A state ruled by the wealthy or wealthy class. It is a form of an oligarchy because the wealthy class is typically the minority. In many plutocratic societies, it's those who dominate ownership of land, natural resources, and government contracts that rule the roost.

Writer Noam Chomsky believes the United States resembles a plutocracy, but that's because he's an idiot communist. He hates capitalism and idealizes the pie-in-the-sky view of communism while simultaneously ignoring its murder of millions. After all, atheist-promoting communist systems killed more than 100 million people in the last century.

Wealth, no doubt, plays a role in the U.S. political system. The rich elite of New York and Washington do have more influence than the plumber and waitress in Wichita. To deny that is to deny gravity. But keeping our eye on the prize, we must admit that the U.S. system still continues to protect individual rights (although religious ones are quickly being eroded), maintain a balance of power, and preserve the freedom to participate in the political process regardless of the party in power—certainly better than any other system.

Pods

Noun

A groups of kids who gather outside a school system to continue their education, typically at one family's home. This may be led by a parent or hired tutor. Pods are used by parents who choose to deviate from the new "COVID-19 Learning Rules" dictated by the supersmart and all-powerful school executives, mayors, and governors across the country who have delayed the reopening of public schools until after the presidential election or the defending of the police, ostensibly for the health and safety of the children. (I don't know—you explain it.) This sounds a lot like "homeschooling," which is frowned upon by the parents in these social circles, so they call it their "gathering pods" instead, which should not be confused with the storage company that leaves a giant box in your driveway for you to fill up with your useless junk.

Politician (politico)

Noun

A person seeking or holding public office. Basic examination of the word indicates that it's simply a job descriptor. Someone who works with electric elements is an electrician. A person employed in politics is a politician. However, due to the pervasiveness of a professional political class reveling in power, the word "politics" has become unsavory, and "politician" is now the equivalent of a four-letter word.

Consequently, candidates rarely use it to describe themselves but rather launch it as a derogatory accusation against their rivals. Successfully. The high poll numbers of 2016 Republican presidential nonpolitician candidates, businessman Donald Trump and Doctor Ben Carson, illustrate the public's distaste for career deceivers— ahem, politicians.

> *A politician needs the ability to foretell what is going to happen tomorrow, next week, next month, and next year. And to have the ability afterwards to explain why it didn't happen.*
>
> —Winston Churchill

Politics

Noun

Poli comes from the Greek, meaning "many." And *tics* are blood-sucking parasites. The activities associated with the struggle between differences of opinions in the same country about its governance. Politics specifically refers to the debates and posturing toward achieving or thwarting power.

It is also an all-encompassing term for elections, appointments, individual rights, and legislative policies. For leftists, everything is political because politics is the god that will usher in Shangri-la. It is where they find their purpose and meaning, which is why they infuse it into every element of life: race, religion, speech, sex, and Starbucks' cups.

Conservatives are dragged into the political realm because, as Plato said, "One of the penalties for refusing to participate in politics is that you end up being governed by your inferiors."

> *For the Left, politics is the way to transform the world; for conservatives, politics is primarily the way to stop the Left from doing so.*
>
> —Dennis Prager in *Still the Best Hope*

#Politics, #PoliticalGames

Poll

Noun

The place where we exercise our most sacrosanct of rights: voting. A poll is also the recording of opinions to ascertain a consensus; first ever official poll was taken in Pennsylvania in 1824.

With each election cycle, media outlets inundate their reporting and commentary with poll numbers. Candidates tout their climbs and dismiss their declines. Percentage points and margin of error become common vernacular, and tongue twisters "Rasmussen" and "Quinnipiac" are spun like silk. However, despite their frequent citations, polls can be biased, and it's important to dissect *how* the questions were asked and of *whom* they were asked. The polls for the 2016 elections all wrongly predicted British citizens' rejection of Brexit and Hillary Clinton's win, strangely things the mainstream media and leftists desperately desired. For this reason, people have grown increasingly distrusting of polls of late.

> *Leadership cannot be measured in a poll or even in the result of an election. It can only be truly seen with the benefit of time. From the perspective of 20 years, not 20 days.*
>
> —Marco Rubio

Poverty line

Noun

The income level the Census Bureau uses to determine who and how many are below the government's designated standard of living. Introduced in the 1960s, it is defined by comparing pretax income against a dollar amount considered a poverty threshold and adjusted for family size. When classifying people as "below the poverty line," the Census Bureau omits noncash welfare benefits, such as healthcare, social services, education and training, and housing. Nor does it include paid Social Security or tax credits, which skews the results of the Census.

The term "poverty" conjures up images of starving, homelessness, and destitution. However, the majority of those categorized as "living below the poverty line" do not represent that. Many own their own three-bedroom, one-and-a-half-bath, with a porch or patio homes. They also have cars, air conditioning, a washer and dryer, a microwave, two TVs, cable, healthcare, and money to meet essential needs and are not hungry. They may not live lavish lifestyles, but they are not the poverty-stricken indigents liberals make them out to be. Leftists use this term to tug at taxpayer heartstrings and garner support for more government intervention.

There are poor people in America. But if poor means the inability to work and a lack of warm housing, nutritious food, and clothing, then there are relatively few "below the poverty line" that fit into that category. Many of them spend the same (adjusted for inflation) as those who made the median income in the 1970s. True poverty is heartbreaking, but the government's definition is not accurate.

Pragmatism

Noun

A logical, rational approach to problem solving.

Idealism is noble. Success is built on big dreams. Innovation arises out of dreams. Love, hope, and charity are found in the untouchable realm of souls. But without pragmatism, none of them would come to fruition. When devising a policy, a very simple question must follow: "And then what?" Rational consideration of consequences is paramount. Applying the "if, then" rule of logic is a good starting point.

Let's take Obamacare as an example. The pragmatist, considering the options, suggests that if we mandate that only specific health insurance policies be offered, then millions of people will be kicked off their plans. *They will get new plans.*

To which a pragmatist would follow up with, "Will they be able to afford the new plans?" *Many of them will not.*

How, then, will they pay for it? *Government subsidies.*

So those who *could* afford the health insurance they *wanted* will now have a plan they don't want, paid for by taxpayers.

This does not seem prudent or wise. Perhaps we should keep thinking.

In the example of Obamacare, reason, foreseeable consequences, and rules of logic were thrown out the window, and thus a catastrophic overhaul of the U.S. healthcare system ensued, disenfranchising many and leaving tens of millions still uninsured.

What good is an idealistic vision without pragmatism? No good at all.

You see, idealism detached from action is just a dream. But idealism allied with pragmatism, with rolling up your sleeves and making the world bend a bit, is very exciting. It's very real. It's very strong.

—Bono, Irish singer/songwriter, philanthropist

#Pragmatism, #ThinkBeforeYouAct

Primary or primary election

Noun

Preliminary to the presidential election, choosing a party candidate or electing the delegates to a party conference.

Presidential primaries occur from February to June of the election year. Success in the first few—Iowa (caucus), New Hampshire, South Carolina—tends to carry the most weight, giving the candidates advantages in publicity and fundraising. They can be "open," meaning any registered voter can vote in the party primary regardless of their affiliation, or "closed," meaning only voters registered with the party can vote in that party's primary.

Think of primary elections as episodes of *American Idol*. For months the candidates pound the pavement, hone their messaging, and try to put their best foot forward (sometimes they stick it in their mouths). The viewers vote, and someone goes home. With each episode/election, the field typically dwindles until a clear party nominee emerges. Although given the maneuvering, mudslinging, and backbiting, perhaps *Survivor* is a better analogy.

#2020Primary, #2020Election

Printing press

Noun

A machine for printing text, invented in 1440 by Johannes Gutenberg. Prior to this world-changing innovation, all written words had to be laboriously copied by hand, which severely limited the availability of books. The printing press allowed for mass reproduction of texts, making them accessible to all classes of people and encouraging literacy. With this new market of printed materials, ideas spread on a scale never seen before. The printing press became the Internet of the 15th century. Now, YouTube and other web avenues offer even wider distribution of nonliterary information, which opens an entirely new paradigm for the thoughtful exchange of ideas.

> *You can't have an industrial revolution, you can't have democracies, you can't have populations who can govern themselves until you have literacy. The printing press simply unlocked literacy.*
> —Howard Rheingold

President

Noun

The highest political position available in our Republic. In the United States, the president serves in a four-year term and is limited to two terms, as stated in the 22nd Amendment to our Constitution. Article 2 of the Constitution outlines his or her requirements and duties.

The president of the United States is the head of the executive branch of government and ceremonial head of state, as well as the commander in chief. He or she is the face and voice of the most successful and powerful nation in history. Therefore, his or her positions, tone, and actions have far-reaching ramifications. Ronald Reagan's strength helped destroy communism; Barack Obama's weakness fostered the growth of ISIS.

The president's power is checked by the legislative and judicial branches of government. His or her job is not to make laws but to oversee enforcement—even for the ones he or she does not like. President Obama famously said, "I'm the president of the United States, not the emperor of the United States." If only he behaved as if he believed that. He also said, "I've got a pen and a phone," implying that he could always use executive power if Congress failed to please him. Congress applauded his overreaches. Evidencing this "my way or the highway" attitude, Obama encouraged a general disregard for laws that appeared contrary to his purposes, especially with regard to persons entering the United States illegally.

Donald Trump took action during the early days of the COVID-19 pandemic to suspend travel from China to the United States, for which Democrats roundly criticized him. Then he was derided for not issuing federal U.S.-wide proclamations that were ultimately beyond his purview. He encouraged the governors to deal with their states individually, as the system was designed. The president's power is limited, but it seems we must hope that he recognizes that as much as everyone else.

#ExecutiveBranch, #ImperialPresident, #ExecutiveActions, #ExecutiveOrders

Progressive

Adjective/noun

The newest in a litany of pseudonyms for leftism and leftists employed to obscure the true nature of this deceitful, evil ideology. Don't allow yourself to be fooled by the changing names. Progressive = Marxist = Leftist = Socialist = Communist = Democratic Socialist = Collectivist. Favoring liberal social reforms that are often tragically backward, a progressive typically believes that he or she knows better for others than they themselves can possibly know, although he or she also typically lacks any relevant education or experience.

Progressivism was a sociopolitical movement beginning more than 100 years ago. Initially focused on the plight of the poor, oppressed, and underprivileged, it eventually vested its faith in government intervention—for everything. Today, this "compassionate" and "free-thinking" movement supports murdering babies in the womb, assisted suicide of the ill and elderly, speech banning, and quashing religious (but only Christian) rights. This is progress?

Even their love affair with wealth redistribution is old and tired; Robin Hood was stealing from the rich to give to the poor long before Bernie Sanders' and Alexandria Ocasio-Cortez's wild-eyed rants. Karl Marx loved the idea so much that he stole it, because collectivists believe they should own everything. Of course, Marx's ideas also failed. All of western Europe ripped a page out of his manifesto, and now the nations of the European Union are crumbling in economic despair. Despite every example of failure, American progressives still peddle the same rotten tripe. So, really, progressives aren't forward thinking; they're just corrupt thieves hell-bent on convincing everyone else to put them in power.

Bernie Sanders ran on raising taxes on the 1 percent to pay their "fair share." Then he became part of the 1 percent. When asked if he would pay more in taxes, *he laughed.* "Pfft . . . come on. . . . I am. I paid the taxes that I owe." Progressives don't actually believe their own lies; they just peddle them.

Steven Spielberg said, "If the world ran the way a crew runs a set, we'd have a better, more progressive world," revealing the utter dishonesty of these charlatans. But the United States *does* run like a movie set, that is, a meritocracy. Steven Spielberg makes millions of dollars on a movie, while a production assistant's salary is roughly $600 a week. If Steven Speilberg really wanted a *progressive* world, he would give at least half of his salary to the PA. But from his point of view, a set runs more like a dictatorship—with him at the head—just the way he likes it. Economies cannot be run that way.

Progressives are privileged elitists who convince the ignorant masses to throw temper tantrums about minimum wage, college tuition, and microaggressions as they whine and demand that schools, government, and the 1 percenters owe them. In reality, progressives fight to regress—into childhood and the inevitable mistakes of repeated history.

> *Those who cannot remember the past are condemned to repeat it.*
> —George Santayana

#Progressive, #ProgressiveFail, #Leftist, #Socialist

Pro tem

Adverb

An abbreviated version of the Latin phrase *pro tempore*, meaning "for the time being." It's a person who stands in for an official who is absent. The U.S. Senate pro tem was created in Article 1, Section 3, of the Constitution and acts as president of the Senate (the vice president of the United States) when he or she is absent and, in theory, presides over sessions. However, more often than not, that duty is given to junior senators to offer them parliamentary experience. The Senate pro tem is usually the most senior senator of the majority party and third in line for succession to the presidency.

Pundit

Noun

An expert on a subject who unpacks and expresses his or her arguments and opinions via radio, television, or the writing of columns or books.

Punditry has exploded over the last two decades. With the 24-hour news cycle of Fox News, MSNBC, CNN, and the wide array of radio shows and Internet outlets, everyone has become an "expert" with an opinion. Unfortunately, those labeled "pundits" are not all experts, and many do not have logical or rational support for their commentaries.

> *If you go and talk to most people, they mean well but they don't have much of a breadth on education, of knowledge, or understanding of what the real issues are and therefore they listen to pundits on television who tell them what they are supposed to think and they keep repeating that until pretty soon they say, "Oh, well that must be true."*
>
> —Ben Carson

#Pundits, #Media

Q/QAnon

Noun

Starting as recently as 2017 with a prediction on 4chan about the imminent arrest of Hillary Clinton (that proved to be false), the Q movement is founded on the fundamental beliefs that life should be valued and patriotism is good. QAnons (the *anon* stands for "anonymity") hold that the "deep state" is involved in a massive child sex-trafficking ring. And with the suspicious media lockstep deriding this vast right-wing conspiracy theory, the Qs might have a point. (See also **Pizzagate** and **Drain the swamp**.)

#QAnon, #Pizzagate, #DraintheSwamp

Quarantine

Noun

When people are sick, they are isolated as a way of preventing the infection of others and guarding against their further exposure to elements that might be hazardous to their weakened health.

In the case of COVID-19 and in the interest of "fairness," the leftists called for quarantining the healthy. Scientifically, it makes zero sense, but from the viewpoint of Amazon, Walmart, Target, and all the net-streaming companies, which, coincidentally, are affiliated with the news media—it makes business sense. Shut down the small businesses by calling them hazardous while leaving open the larger chain stores that offer the same goods and services, with more people and more contact points. Keep people at home so they can watch the advertising.

There's a reason it's called television programming.

A ton of propaganda ensued from the lockdown. What is ignored is that the quarantine is also *hazardous* to the health of the nation, fiscally, mentally, and physically—perhaps worse than the disease.

> *But this is not a major threat to people of the United States and this is not something that the citizens of the United States right now should be worried about.*
>
> —Anthony Fauci, White House Coronavirus Task Force
> member and medical adviser, January 21, 2020

Quid pro quo

Noun

Latin for "this for that." While this term can refer to a simple business transaction, politicians have employed it to imply inappropriate demands or favors used as leverage. Two recent examples are as follows:

1. Vice President Joe Biden threatened to withhold a billion dollars in aid from the United States until President Poroshenko of Ukraine fired his investigator for looking into Burisma, an energy company that was paying Hunter Biden, Joe's son, between $50,000 and $85,000 per month. In a video-recorded presentation, Biden Sr. boasted about how the president acceded to his wishes: "I'm leaving in six hours. If the prosecutor is not fired, you're not getting the money. Well, son of a b-tch. (Laughter.) He got fired."

2. President Donald Trump had a phone conversation with the new President Zelensky of Ukraine and suggested he look into the corruption, including that of Biden, that seemed rampant in his country. For instance, Obama sent them several billion dollars that simply went missing. At the time they spoke, there were aid funds that were still in process, destined to the Ukraine. For this phone call, the president

was derided for instituting a quid pro quo, which both he and President Zelensky deny ever happened, mainly because there was no investigation and the funds were released as planned. If there is no quid, there can be no quo.

Quota

Noun

A fixed amount to be fulfilled, owed, or contributed. Quotas are great for manufacturing lines of material fashioned by a machine: 100 widgets per hour. Quotas for widgets reveal the productivity of the workers, but not the productivity of the widget.

Proponents of quotas for minorities in schools and businesses view people as widgets—a statistic or number by which they show the world their concern. But quotas often impose falsehoods and champion special, *unearned* treatment.

In the 1978 ruling in *Regents of University of California v. Bakke*, the Supreme Court deemed quotas in university entrants unconstitutional. However, it did uphold that universities may still consider race as a factor in admitting applicants. (So they can secretly use quotas as long as they don't *call* them quotas.)

An even more outrageous example came when the Obama administration pressured some public schools to enact racial quota punishment limits. Minneapolis public schools agreed to lessen the gap in punishment of black students by 25 percent by the end of 2014, 50 percent the next year, then 75 and 100 percent in the following years. Oh, to be a black student in the Minneapolis school district. The dog would eat my homework every day. Boys I disliked would have an eraser thrown at their head every session. Teachers pushing a liberal agenda would be called foolish, idiotic, and spawns of the devil with reckless abandon.

Some people believe that imposing arbitrary quotas on delinquency issues led to the Parkland school shooting where 14 young people and 3 teachers died.

Quotas devalue individual worth by placing skin color, gender, or another superficiality above intelligence, ambition, and skill. They are political ploys, counterproductive to a qualified individual's chance to better himself or herself and detrimental to the person who advances unfairly because of superficial values rather than talent and ability.

I don't believe in quotas. America was founded on a philosophy of individual rights, not group rights.

—Supreme Court Justice Clarence Thomas

Racist

Adjective, noun

Exhibiting or believing that a person's skin color or race primarily determines his or her abilities. Judging a book by its cover. A racist makes assumptions solely based on appearances. And to assume makes an "ass" of "u" and "me." The Left has coopted the word to bludgeon and silence people because it is virtually indefensible. There is no way to effectively prove you are not racist.

The national media have highlighted race and racism in the United States, and the 1619 project proposes that we were founded by African slavers (not in 1776, with the Declaration of Independence), whose sins have forever tarnished this great nation beyond redemption. They casually forget the Civil War, fought by whites and blacks to free slaves. They easily ignore that black Africans trafficked in slavery and black African Americans owned slaves. They ignore the estimated 9.2 million black slaves currently in Africa (according to the Global Slave Index). That's because their focus is not to correct former injustice. It is to tear down freedom. The Left practices its own form of racism—a racism of thought. As it appropriated the term to attack its enemies, it embraces an ideology of hate that differs little from actual racism.

> *The point I was making was not that Grandmother harbors any racial animosity. She doesn't. But she is a typical white person.*
>
> —Barack Obama

> *Hating people because of their color is wrong. And it doesn't matter which color does the hating. It's just plain wrong.*
>
> —Muhammad Ali

Radical

Adjective

An individual who fights for and desires to see extreme change, unlike anything that has come before it. Depending on context, the term "radical" can be applied as a compliment or a criticism.

Radical Muslims have employed kidnapping, bombing, rape, and torture in their attempts to attain their stated desire for a world under the rule of Sharia law.

America's revolutionaries were also radical. Prior to this new Republic they fought to create, authoritarian monarchies, theocracies, and dictators dominated our collective history. A representative government with separated powers was a truly radical idea.

> *When you are right, you cannot be too radical; when you are wrong, you cannot be too conservative.*
>
> —Martin Luther King, Jr.

Dr. King and his fellow civil rights fighters also represent the positive connotation of the term. The treatment of blacks under segregation and Jim Crow laws was abominable. Radical change was needed.

In some cases, the label is both heralded and rebuked. The radical leftists of the 1960s—the Black Panthers, Weather Underground, and Saul Alinksy followers—stormed college administration buildings, stoked racial riots, bombed buildings, and shot police officers because they viewed American society as oppressive and poisonous. They wore radical as a badge of honor. But these violent, hysterical agitators pursued destruction of what America's original radical revolutionaries created.

History is repeating itself on college campuses today with protests and shrieking demands to limit, and even ban, speech. Revoking the First Amendment is indeed radical. But it is not sane.

#Radical, #RadicalIslam, #Extremism

Reactionary

Adjective

The extremes (in terms of people) of different political sides. Reactionaries have knee-jerk, emotion-based responses, and they exist on both the right and left sides of the aisle. However, just because one calls another reactionary does not make it so. It is often used incorrectly as a condescending term to dismiss an opposing point of view. If the argument is logical, rational, and on point, to call it reactionary is disingenuous. Given that the Left is far more driven by emotion-based rationale, the "reactionary" label affixes accurately to them more than to those on the right. Here are a few examples of reactionary views from the left:

- A crazy or evil man uses an illegal gun to murder people.
  - Liberals shout for more gun control to inhibit purchases by law-abiding citizens.
- Computer weather models predict temperature increases (that observable data refute).
  - Reform the entire world economy with the Green New Deal.
- A black criminal attacking a police officer is killed.
  - Rioters burn down cities and birth a movement encouraging violence and the murder of police officers.

The limitation of riots, moral questions aside, is that they cannot win and their participants know it. Hence rioting is not revolutionary but reactionary because it invites defeat. It involves an emotional catharsis, but it must be followed by a sense of futility.

—Martin Luther King, Jr.

Recession

Noun

A temporary decline in the economy, specifically defined by two consecutive quarters of negative economic growth in the gross domestic product (GDP). The United States has experienced seven recessions since 1960. They can last from a few months to a few years—as was the case in the Great Depression of the 1930s.

Approaches to recovery make all the difference in the world. President Reagan pushed tax cuts as encouragement for people to work, spend, save, and invest after Jimmy Carter's failed policies ground our economy to a screeching halt. The year the cuts were fully implemented in 1983, the economy grew by 7.6 percent.

In response to the 2008–2009 recession, President Obama chose to increase government spending, called "the stimulus," and as a result, we experienced the absolute weakest recovery of all six prior post-Depression recoveries. The average cumulative growth of GDP for those was over 25 percent, whereas in 2015 it reached just over 13 percent, or half as much. Also, the president appointed Joe Biden in charge of the $737 billion, and no one has seen it since.

Recession is when your neighbor loses his job. Depression is when you lose yours. And recovery is when Jimmy Carter loses his.

—Ronald Reagan

Americans know that we cannot tax and spend our way out of a recession, yet Democrats can't grasp this simple fact.

—Pete Sessions

#Recession, #Markets, #Indicators

Red tape

Noun

The colloquial phrase for excessive bureaucratic government regulations and control: city or state agencies or officials requiring endless forms, licenses, committee approvals, filings, inspections, and investigations.

Red tape is government run amok, seeking self-justification. The more rules they write, the greater is the need for enforcement. Adding insult to injury, most regulations are edicts; they are not passed by any legislature and are written by unelected officials (thus allowing elected officials to officially denounce the regulations without taking responsibility for them!).

Overwhelming red tape inhibits people from starting businesses and impedes smaller businesses from competing with larger ones because of the excessive costs to maintain compliance. Challenging red tape typically results in delays, fines, rejections, lawsuits, or, alas . . . more regulations. Red tape is a boot on the neck of American citizens. It discourages innovation and kills opportunity. All that tape would be better used to bind the hands of bureaucratic officials.

> *The sooner we rein in the red tape factory in Washington, DC, the sooner small businesses can get back to creating jobs and helping more Americans find an honest day's work.*
>
> —Geoff Davis, congressional representative, Kentucky

#RedTape, #Bureaucracy

Referendum

Noun

A direct vote by the electorate to approve or repeal a policy or law passed by the legislature. There is generally a 90-day period in which the people must gather signatures on a petition to place the referendum up for a popular vote.

In the United States, referendums serve only at state and local levels. They illustrate the form of democracy where laws are made by the people. For example, in 2013, the California legislature passed a bill allowing students in public schools to choose which bathroom or locker room to use based on which gender they "identified" as, regardless of their biological sex. Many Californians believed it was dangerous and infringed on others' rights to privacy and gained enough support to place a referendum up for a vote to block the law. However, bureaucrats deemed one-fifth of the signatures invalid and claimed additional signatures arrived too late.

Referendum is also more broadly used as a philosophical description of public approval of an elected candidate or party. For instance, in 2010, Republicans overwhelmingly swept the midterm House elections. The voters were fed up with the Democrats' leftist direction and used the ballot box to express their desire to change the shape and trajectory of the nation.

> *2010 is not just a choice between Republicans and Democrats.*
> *2010 is not just a choice between liberals and conservatives.*
> *2010 is a referendum on the very identity of our nation.*
> —Marco Rubio

Religion

Noun

An individual's worldview; a belief system of faith and worship. Worldwide, Christianity boasts the most adherents, followed by Islam and then Hinduism. According to Wikipedia, atheism and agnosticism have recently entered the field. Together they comprise *irreligion* or *secular humanism*.

Religion offers a philosophy that shapes behavior and purpose in society. It gives us our morality, which is why when a politician says, "I won't base my political decision on my religion," run for the hills, because that's a hypocrite. For instance, pro-choice Nancy

Pelosi claims to be a Catholic, though the Catholic church stands firmly against abortion.

The Left likes to criticize religion—well, Christianity anyway; Islam is just fine and dandy—but leftism itself has become a religion, albeit a secular one. Its faith is in the federal or world government. Which is funny, because that is placing one's faith in *man*, and the argument of the Left is that *man* is fallible and the *state* must retain power!

Our representative Republic is the best government ever formed in the world, where power resides in the *individual* because, collectively, each person making his or her own decisions harnesses and magnifies individual creativity and ingenuity to the advantage of all. The United States produced the greatest leap in prosperity the world has ever seen, to the benefit of the entire world, but the secular humanists would destroy all that to concentrate power in the hands of so few . . . and among them, so many nonproducer idiots!

#Religion, #Christianity, #Hinduism, #Islam

Rent control

Noun

A government-instituted rental regulation that restricts landlords from increasing rent. Intended to help the poor, instead it only buries them deeper by stunted inflation. Rent control is often mistakenly presented as a way for poor tenants to fight greedy landlords. But many elites in rent-controlled buildings hoard their apartments and pay well below the market rate for years, even decades. Price "controls" create shortages—an excess of demand over supply, which then encourages higher noncontrolled housing prices. San Francisco and New York have rent control, as well as the country's highest real estate values.

Rent control also allows current tenants to shift other costs to future tenants and non-rent-controlled owners. When landlords are forced to keep rent low, they are then able to get their property assessment lowered. Lower property values render lower property taxes, forcing those with higher values to subsidize the rent-controlled properties.

Rent control may help a few low-income folks, but it prevents other low-income and middle-class people from living in a city that without rent control would be vastly more affordable. Who gets to decide the pricing? Elite bureaucrats!

Rent seeker

Noun

A term coined by economist Anne Krueger (managing director of the International Monetary Fund), it is a business using political means to gain benefits, typically through subsidies or a regulation that restricts competition.

For instance, a labor union spends a million dollars lobbying the government to stop right-to-work laws and compel union membership and then recoups the million dollars and more from compulsory union dues. Its efforts also restrict current or potential marketplace competition by any company that cannot afford to pay union wages. The labor *union* may profit, but the workers and overall economy suffer.

The same is true for an industry seeking subsidies. If an agricultural company spends a million dollars lobbying, that is a million dollars not being used to create more wealth by expanding, investing in innovation, hiring more employees, or raising wages. Instead, it is simply exchanged for a different million dollars that comes from the government—that is, taxpayers.

Rent-seeking behavior invariably leads to more rent seeking because of the manipulation of the free-market system and the restriction of competition to enter the market. Competition benefits the consumer, and rent seeking stifles competition through bureaucratic overreach.

Republic

Noun

The term is used broadly to describe over a hundred nations that vary in political ideologies. It is commonly applied simply to exclude the presence of a monarchy. The United States is called a republic, but so is Sudan, the People's Republic of China, and the former United Soviet Socialist Republic. James Madison wrote about such usage in Federalist No. 39: "These examples, which are nearly as dissimilar to each other as to a genuine republic, shew the extreme inaccuracy with which the term has been used in political disquisitions."

The roots of a republic are found in ancient Greece, but our Founders realized that in addition to the excellent aspects, there were also deficiencies. They did not abandon it but rather improved upon it. Madison clarified further: "a government which derives all its powers directly or indirectly from the great body of the people." Although a defining characteristic is representative government, the central element of a republic is the separation of powers. Without that component, a government of the people would quickly devolve into a mob-ruled democracy.

President Obama's defiance and overstepping of his constitutional authority reveal Benjamin Franklin's astute wisdom in 1787. At the close of the Constitutional Convention, Mrs. Powell of Philadelphia asked him, "What kind of government have you given us, Dr. Franklin? A monarch or a republic?"

To which Franklin replied, "A republic, if you can keep it."

#Republic, #WeThePeople

Republican

Noun

A member of the Republican Party. Originated in 1854 by anti-slavery activists, the Republican Party, also known as the Grand

Old Party or GOP, elected the first Republican president, Abraham Lincoln in 1860, a mere six years later.

The philosophy of the Republican Party is rooted in personal responsibility, individual liberty, limited government, free enterprise, and constitutionalism. Stances on fiscal issues such as taxes, trade, and spending, as well as the social issues of abortion, affirmative action, and the preservation of traditional marriage, all grow from the root. Whether religious or secular, Republicans know that America's fundamentals are based on the Judeo-Christian belief that humans are not inherently good and therefore must be accountable to a higher moral framework. Eschewing personal accountability precipitates selfishness and narcissism. If one doesn't believe that laws are good and valuable, nothing will make him or her abide by the law, save brute force. Sacrificing the mainstream belief in a supernatural God necessitates an authoritarian godlike state instead, and morality becomes malleable because whoever is in power gets to decide its limitations or lack thereof.

Sadly, some in the GOP have foundered and succumbed to the idea of government as god. These folks have garnered the moniker RINO—Republican in Name Only. They espouse the rhetoric but do not adhere to the actual principles of the party.

Republicans are historically strong and steadfast like their elephant symbol denotes. Because elephants have superb memories, they are able to employ their knowledge to analyze what is safe and beneficial. Republicans do the same. Democrats, on the other hand, are represented by a donkey. And they've got everything ass-backward!

I am a Republican, a black, dyed in the wool Republican, and I never intend to belong to any other party than the party of freedom and progress.

—Frederick Douglass, former slave, statesman

#Republican, #GOP, #Principled

Repatriation

Noun

The process of returning material to its country of origin. It applies to immigrants, cultural objects like art, and foreign earnings being brought back to the home nation of the business.

Until recently, a U.S. business operating overseas would pay tax to the country it was operating in *and* to the IRS—in the amount of 35 percent—if the company repatriated the profit back to the United States. Recently, with the enactment of Donald Trump's 2017 Tax Cuts and Jobs Act, over a billion dollars has been repatriated to the United States. Corporations have deployed those funds for further investment and expansion in the United States.

> *President Barack Obama had long decried the practice of companies shifting profits abroad, though he and his party proposed to add taxes and penalties to "unpatriotic" companies, rather than changing taxes and regulations to create new incentives to invest at home.*
>
> —Joel Pollack, editor, Breitbart News

> *[Trump says] he's going to bring all these jobs back. Well how exactly are you going to do that? What are you going to do? . . . What magic wand do you have?*
>
> —Barack Obama

Answer: Repatriation.

#Repatriation, #Repatriate

Rule of law

Noun

A written form of rules all are expected to obey or be subject to punishments, eliminating any allowance for arbitrary exercise of power. The rule of law cannot be changed willy-nilly based on views of "social justice." Laws must be changed through legislation, not through the executive or judicial branches.

Liberals fervently reject the rule of law. In the confirmation hearings for Justice Samuel Alito, Democrats were not concerned with the proper execution of jurisprudence but instead focused on "favoring the little guy." Democratic Senator Herb Kohl stated, "The neutral approach, that of the judge just applying the law, is very often inadequate to ensure social progress."

Fellow Democratic Senator Richard Durbin said, "it raises the question in my mind whether the average person, the dispossessed person, the poor person who finally has their day in court . . . [is] going to be subject to the crushing hand of fate when it comes to your decisions."

Their objections had nothing to do with the rule of law and whether or not Justice Alito would uphold it. Democrats also vigorously opposed Justice Kavanaugh's appointment, based on the highly questionable and completely unverifiable testimony of Christine Blasey Ford, who claimed he had sexually assaulted her in high school, 35 years prior. The leftist campaign to #BelieveHer (without evidence) will hypocritically not extend to Joe Biden's accuser.

Justice is supposed to be blind. The law should be agenda free. Favoring "equality" over justice is a nail in the coffin of a free society. The court's job is to adjudicate, not seek social change. In a court of law, there should be no special treatment or consideration for the poor, just as there should be none for the rich.

Two things form the bedrock of any open society—freedom of expression and rule of law. If you don't have those things, you don't have a free country.

—Salman Rushdie

Safe seat

Noun

A legislative seat that is protected by a large majority vote.

It's often argued that seats are safe due to gerrymandering and rearranging district lines to give one party an advantage, capturing areas that skew one party over another. While this may be true in some instances, there are also areas that will always sway one way regardless of district lines. For instance, California's 12th district (San Francisco) has been held by a Democrat since 1949, and current office holder Nancy Pelosi won with 80 percent of the vote.

Politicians in safe seats rest easy knowing they will not face a serious opponent and therefore only continue to feed their "base" and ignore dissent, thereby ensuring support for their next election. The more safe seats, the less likely representatives will change their behavior. If they know they just can't lose, they just don't care.

Second Amendment

Noun

> A well-regulated militia being necessary to the security of a free state, the right of the people to keep and bear arms shall not be infringed.

The Second Amendment to the United States Constitution was ratified as part of the Bill of Rights on December 15, 1791. These declarations distinctly protected specific rights of the individual citizens of the country such that the government could not mistakenly impose its will on the people. Many people make the mistake of thinking that the Bill of Rights *grants* rights. Nope. It simply preserves them, lest there be any doubt.

More recently, the gun grabbers and power seekers want to take this Second Amendment right away, arguing that it is unnecessary (to them, surely). They claim the Framers intended guns for hunting, but the text clearly refers to a civilian militia—a fighting force. And a government with better weapons than its citizens is a danger to them.

A final word on *infringed*. This means encroached upon in any way. To be absolutely clear, the text is written distinctly that in *no way* shall a citizen's rights to any firepower (that is meaningful in a military context) be compromised.

And that's why there is a new push to declare the Constitution itself outdated and corrupt. (See **Systemic racism**.)

> *What country can preserve its liberties if their rulers are not warned from time to time that their people preserve the spirit of resistance? Let them take arms.*
>
> —Thomas Jefferson

Secretary of state

Noun

A member of the president's cabinet and the highest position in the State Department, responsible for the tone and policy of foreign affairs. The State Department's website lists the following as some of the secretary's duties:

- Serves as the president's principal adviser on U.S. foreign policy
- Conducts negotiations relating to U.S. foreign affairs
- Ensures the protection of the U.S. government to American citizens, property, and interests in foreign countries

- Informs the Congress and American citizens on the conduct of U.S. foreign relations

Former Secretary Hillary Clinton fumbled the ball on all of the above. On her watch, four Americans, including our Ambassador Chris Stevens, were murdered at the consulate in Benghazi, Libya. The British had evacuated, after an assassination attempt on their ambassador, and the Red Cross had been attacked, yet Clinton's State Department denied Steven's multiple requests for more security. There are myriad theories as to why, focusing on some clandestine arms dealings between our government and terrorist thugs. Those remain unproven.

After the attack on our embassy, Clinton followed that dereliction by failing to correctly inform Congress and citizens about the conduct of her foreign relations. She lied about the attack, calling it a spontaneous uprising and blaming an Internet video for causing it, and then when called to testify before Congress defended her inaction and lies with the glib and callous, "What difference, at this point, does it make?" Susan Rice, then ambassador to the United Nations, and even President Obama joined the chorus in blaming a harmless Internet video for inciting the violence in Benghazi.

Q: What did Hillary do in Benghazi?

A: Nothing. The H is silent in Benghazi.

A notable accomplishment of Clinton's time as secretary was her presentation of the "Russian reset" button to Russian Foreign Minister Sergei Lavrov. Clinton naively asked him if the translation was right, to which he answered, "You got it wrong." His was an understatement. "Peregruzka," the word she put on the button, means "to overcharge." The intention itself was idiotic. Diplomacy with an adversary cannot be accomplished by handing them a plastic button.

Hillary's successor, John Kerry, continued the trend of incompetent negligence. While U.S. Marine Sgt. Andrew Tahmoorisi was wrongfully held in a Mexican prison, 90,000 children were flowing across the southern border, Syria's president was killing hundreds of thousands of his own people, Iraq was crumbling, and ISIS was murdering their way through the Middle East, Kerry was speaking at an "Our Ocean" conference. He believes climate change is as big of a threat as terrorism and is creating climate refugees. Nobody has ever met a single one of those, but there are 900,000 terror refugees flooding into Europe and the United States.

The secretary of state's job is, first and foremost, to live in reality—the cold, hard reality that the world is a dangerous place, and he or she has a primary role in keeping America safe from those who threaten us.

#SecretaryofState, #RussianReset, #IranDeal

Secular humanism

Noun

Also known as anti-Christianism. Likely the most murderous worldview known to mankind. Secular humanism is the religion of the communist state and the worldview that is currently taught in our U.S. education system. It maintains that all life is accidental (therefore, valueless) and Darwin was right; that is, *survival of the fittest* is the law of the land. Oh, and by the way, they also try to teach, antithetically, no bullying! (Unless you disagree, in which case you are targeted with vitriol, ridicule, and even violence.) Incidentally, even Darwin didn't believe his theory and said as much in his renowned 1859 book, *On the Origin of Species.*

> *To suppose that the eye, with all its inimitable contrivances for adjusting the focus to different distances, for admitting different amounts of light, and for the correction of spherical and chromatic aberration, could have been formed by natural selection, seems, I freely confess, absurd in the highest possible degree.*
>
> —Charles Darwin, *On the Origin of Species*

Senate

Noun

The smaller upper assembly of the U.S. Congress, comprised of 100 members (two senators from each of 50 states) who each serve a six-year term. Voting ties in the Senate are broken by the president of the Senate, the vice president of the United States.

The Senate, with its several committees, subcommittees, and joint committees, has a separate set of guidelines and procedures than its sister chamber, the House of Representatives.

There are majority and minority leaders, voted on by the members of the respective parties. They seek to unify their parties on legislation, which is vital in passing necessary bills but also destructive when using threats or promising favors to garner a vote. (See **Party-line voting**.)

When they actually vote, that is. The Senate has become a maze of rules upon procedures upon maneuvers. The senators certainly like to stand on the floor and talk a lot, lambasting one another, typically the opposing party. The wheels of justice may move slowly, but the wheels of legislation have completely fallen off. Which is, incidentally, just how the Founders envisioned it, because laws should really be unnecessary.

> *Our Constitution was made only for a moral and religious people. It is wholly inadequate to the government of any other.*
>
> —John Adams

> *If you're hanging around with nothing to do and the zoo is closed, come over to the Senate. You'll get the same kind of feeling and you won't have to pay.*
>
> —Bob Dole

#Senate, #USSenate

Separation of powers

Noun

Separating the major bodies of government power: legislative, judicial, and executive, which helps prevent coercion and abuse of power and is maintained by a system of checks and balances. (See **Checks and balances.**)

The Founders understood the basics of human nature: flawed, fallible, and sinful. Ultimate power in the hands of one person or group of people is dangerous because greed, self-righteousness, and power preservation inevitably take hold. The reason for and importance of separation of powers were best described by James Madison in Federalist No. 51:

> It may be a reflection on human nature, that such devices should be necessary to control the abuses of government. But what is government itself but the greatest of all reflections on human nature? If men were angels, no government would be necessary. If angels were to govern men, neither external nor internal controls on government would be necessary. In framing a government which is to be administered by men over men, the great difficulty lies in this: You must first enable the government to control the governed; and in the next place, oblige it to control itself. A dependence on the people is no doubt the primary control on the government; but experience has taught mankind the necessity of auxiliary precautions.

#SeparationOfPowers, #ChecksAndBalances, #Overreach

Sequester

Noun

Automatic, mandatory, across-the-board cuts in government spending when the deficit is too high, similar to how your mother took away your cell phone the first month you had overage charges.

Initiated to help control spending, the sequester was approved in 2011 to take place in 2013. It was a transparent kick-the-can-down-the-road move. After his reelection, Obama derided the sequester he had installed in 2011, so he tried to derail it. It was strangely as if he never intended to be president in 2013.

Much hoopla was made over Obama's sequester of 2013. Prior to this, Republicans had passed legislation targeting specific cuts, but Democrats insisted on increasing taxes. As a result, Obama approved a uniform percentage cut made across the board. However, the programs that make up 60 percent of the budget—Medicare and Social Security—were exempt from sequestration. And strangely, that same year, the government still found money for these expenditures:

- $1 million for heated pavement at a bus stop in Arlington, Virginia
- $5.4 million on crystal glassware for the Hillary's State Department (how else were they going to drink the $400,000 worth of alcohol?)
- $562,000 for artwork at Veterans Affairs Office (because paintings are far more important than treating the men and women who risk their lives in service to the nation—some of whom died waiting to be seen by a doctor)

The government doesn't have a revenue problem; it has a spending problem. Sequestration occurred because government knows no restraint.

Sequestration is a Band-Aid and Band-Aids don't do a darn bit of good if you're bleeding from an artery. The real problem is irresponsible spending. One of the biggest misunderstandings, or lies, of a sequester is that actual cutting occurs. The 2013 sequester wasn't a cut; it was a reduction in the rate of spending *increases.*

#Sequester, #Sequestration, #BalancedBudget

Serfdom

Noun

The lowest rung on the ladder under feudalism, a political and economic system of the Middle Ages. Serfs, or peasants, worked as slaves in exchange for a lord's protection. They performed the work of farming and were allowed to keep only a fraction of their production, while the rest of it was sent up the chain of feudal command.

Under feudalism, peasants could not own horses, hunt, or cut down trees for firewood. They were not allowed real weapons, could be taxed at any time, and needed their lord's permission for marriage, educating their children, or relocating. The world was a different place in the 1200s: no deadbolt locks on the door, no security cameras, there weren't even streetlights. So, in exchange for their lack of freedom, protection from barbarian pillagers probably seemed like a good deal.

Centuries of industrial and technological progress puts Western society in a very different position. We no longer need the protection the peasants did. But, as Austrian economist Friedrich von Hayek wrote, leftists are willingly running back down *The Road to Serfdom.* The Left ignores the truth that it is the emergence of individual freedom that brought about exponential growth in scientific advancements, material comforts, and general prosperity. The removal of centralized rule ushered in economic fortune for a greater amount of the population. Advocating for more power in the hands of the political "nobility," as Leftists do, is to step toward the servitude of serfdom.

*It is one of the saddest spectacles of our time to see a great demo-
cratic movement support a policy which must lead to the destruction of democracy and which meanwhile can benefit only a
minority of the masses who support it. Yet it is this support from
the Left of the tendencies toward monopoly which make them so
irresistible and the prospects of the future so dark.*

—Friedrich von Hayek

Sexual preference

Noun

The pattern of preference in romantic partners, this typically meant
whether one was straight or gay but later expanded to more fluid
definitions. This was the gentle way to indicate parity in the choice
of hook-ups in our promiscuous society. After Amy Coney Barrett
used the phrase during her Supreme Court confirmation hearings,
Merriam-Webster's online dictionary changed its definition of
the phrase to indicate these words are now considered "offensive."
Seriously!

Why? Because "It's not a choice!" and "I was born this way!"
But these are the same people who argue that one can change biologically from a man to a woman, at will, and what about "My body,
my choice?" The Left holds that one has absolutely no choice in the
way he or she behaves, which holds, if you believe that life formed
in a series of accidents, evolution is true, and death leads to nothing-
ness. But they don't live that way. You can't be at once held accountable for your actions (something they love to do) and simultaneously
considered just a victim of circumstance. According to leftists, your
sexual desires control you, and not the other way around. What a
horrible, childish way to go through life.

To disparage Amy Coney Barrett because she used this phrase is
to disparage someone for saying they prefer vanilla. You can't prefer
vanilla because you can't control what you like! It all feeds into the
victim narrative the Left prefers.

Sharia law

Noun

A comprehensive code that governs the social, personal, political, economic, and legal practices of Muslims. The divine law of Islam. Sharia's primary influence and authority come from the texts of the Quran, the Sunnah, and Hadith. On issues where the Hadith are silent or there is no consensus about a Hadith's authenticity or interpretation, it relies on secondary sources. Some of these differ among the sects of Islam and is why Sharia varies from country to country in the Islamic world.

> *America and Islam are not exclusive and need not be in competition. Instead, they overlap, and share common principles of justice and progress, tolerance and the dignity of all human beings.*
> —Barack Obama

Barack Obama ignores that Sharia is totally incompatible with American views of law and justice. The U.S. Constitution and legal system guarantee and protect fundamental human rights for *all* persons, regardless of religion, sex, or ethnicity. On the contrary, Sharia judges men and women differently. Here are some crimes, punishments, and dictates under Sharia law:

- Apostasy (conversion from Islam)—punishable by death
- Defaming Islam—punishable by death
- Homosexuality—punishable by death
- Theft—punishable by amputation
- Female genital mutilation is required for strict compliance with the law, ostensibly to promote women's chastity.
- Women who are raped can be convicted of unlawful sexual intercourse and lashed or stoned to death unless there are four *male* Muslim witnesses to prove rape.

- A woman's testimony as a witness is equal to half that of a man.
- Men may have up to four wives; women may only have one husband.

Sharia law sees no distinction between church and state. Under Sharia, the church *is* the state.

An Islamist who does not support Sharia would be a hypocrite or a liar.

#Sharia, #ShariaLaw, #RadicalIslam

Shelter-in-place

Adjective

An executive order for citizens to obey, given by overreaching statist governors who were disappointed that President Trump turned out to be much less of a dictator than they had feared/hoped. They turned themselves into the very despots they derided him for being. It meant that citizens were to stay in their home, hiding from the invisible foe of the coronavirus of 2020, which will never go away.

Thanks, China.

#ShelterInPlace, #COVID19

Slate

Noun

A group of candidates who run in multiposition elections on a common platform of a political party or hold similar views on policies. But read those slate mailers carefully. They often make it look like all the candidates are endorsed by the Republican or Democratic Party by slapping an elephant or a donkey on them. However, the logo or presence of candidates does not necessarily mean they are all thinking on the same page. Candidates pay a fee for inclusion on of mailers, and sometimes the company fills the unsold spaces with other candidates whose views might not conform.

Know the candidates because slates are not the most trustworthy of sources.

Smoke-filled room

Noun

United Press journalist Raymond Clapper originated this phrase to describe how Warren G. Harding was nominated as the Republican presidential candidate in 1920. Rumor has it that after a deadlocked convention, Harding was chosen in a private room in the Chicago Blackstone Hotel by a bunch of powerful, cigar-smoking senators. Now the phrase describes private, backdoor political bargaining and meetings conducted by highly influential people instead of open democratic operations.

Social contract

Noun

The theoretical agreement between the people and their government. Individuals consent to give up certain freedoms and be governed in exchange for political order and protection of other rights.

English philosopher Thomas Hobbes is considered the father of the social contract theory. He believed, though, that once the people gave power to the state, they had relinquished any right to it; thus he was a supporter of the monarchy and believed the stronger the government, the better.

Philosopher John Locke built on Hobbes' theory; however, he importantly argued that power was given *conditionally*. If the state fails to satisfy the conditions accompanying its power, it must forfeit that power, which reverts to the citizens. Locke's guiding principle was that the social contract begins with the recognition of human rights: life, liberty, and estate. His philosophy was integral in forming the foundations of America's constitutional Republic.

Sadly, sanctimonious "intellectuals" have hijacked and perverted the term to promote an idea that corporations owe their employees higher wages and government should take care of people from cradle to grave. Increasing wages and paying for others' education, retirement, and healthcare are not what Locke or the Founders intended. The U.S. citizenry has never signed a contract remotely resembling that.

#SocialContract, #JohnLocke

Social engineering

Noun

Influence and persuasion of attitudes and behavior on a large scale; government indoctrination and planning designed to alter citizens' living patterns to ultimately suit its own agenda; the "wise and benevolent" elite devising policies and lecturing the public, typically as if the fate of humanity is at stake.

The Left uses social engineering to force socialist ideals. Using the environment as an excuse, they push expensive endeavors like taxpayer-funded highway bills, rail subsidies, bike paths, and others to engineer, socially, to potentially reduce greenhouse gases. The latest attempt at social engineering is the Green New Deal, which is really the watermelon deal—green on the outside but communist red on the inside.

Determined to force integration of public schools in the 1970s, social engineers insisted on busing minority students into predominately white areas, and vice versa, regardless of how it affected the children, many of whom had to wake up at four or five in the morning to commute across town to strange communities.

Social engineering efforts to change society to suit a utopian ideal are harmful. The forced shaping of thought and behavior is dictatorial. But that is exactly what our public school system has embraced, which is why we see a preponderance of youth lauding socialism and decrying the global warming destruction of the world, which they are taught will occur in fewer than 12 years!

Having federal officials, whether judges, bureaucrats, or congressmen, impose a new definition of marriage on the people is an act of social engineering profoundly hostile to liberty.

—Ron Paul

Social Security

Noun

Federal insurance for retired, elderly, disabled, and low-income people. It is one of the most poorly designed policies in the history of the United States. Hatched in 1935 as one of the many federal welfare programs instituted during the Franklin D. Roosevelt administration, it is a typical liberal feel-good program devised without fully examining the ramifications.

Social Security is funded through payroll taxes collected by the IRS. Roosevelt said, "We have tried to frame a law which will give some measure of protection to the average citizen and to his family against the loss of a job and against poverty-ridden old age." And it did for about 70 years, but it won't in the near future because the very premise of the program was built on sand. It is not a savings or investment plan. It's a Ponzi scheme. Workers never receive the funds that were forcibly taken from their paychecks; that money was used to pay retirees decades ago. In return for their hard-earned money, the government gives them a promise similar to Wimpy's from the Popeye cartoons, "I'll gladly pay you Tuesday for a hamburger today." But some Tuesday in the year 2033, there will be no check because, in its current state, Social Security will be insolvent. The massive baby-boomer generation is retiring, and birth rates are falling; there simply aren't enough people having babies to fund the program. Unless there is a complete restructuring, those in generation X and beyond will never see a penny of the money the government legally stole from them.

The first recipient of Social Security, Ida May Fuller, lived to a 100 years old and collected almost $23,000 from Social Security. The amount she paid into it: $25.75.

#SocialSecurity, #SocialSecurityReform

Socialism

Noun

A political/economic concept based on the theory that if everyone pours everything into the same pot, then everyone will have every-thing—the transitional step from a freer economy to communism. Based on the view that all wealth coagulates in the possession of the few.

Proponents are in love with the *idea* that socialism is for the collective good, which blinds them from the reality that it is nothing of the kind. It kills economic growth by penalizing success while rewarding failure. As French economist Claude-Frédéric Bastiat wrote, "Government is the great fiction through which everybody endeavors to live at the expense of everybody else." It touts "equal-ity" and "compassion," but socialism breeds selfishness and callous-ness, teaching people *not* to take care of others. After all, socialism teaches, that's the government's job.

In Venezuela, the populace reportedly voted for the socialism Hugo Chavez peddled. Now they have no food, no toilet paper, no medicine, and skyrocketing hyperinflation, which means the local currency has no value.

Socialism is like a used car peddled by a slick-talking salesman. He trumpets the paint job, leg room, and how you'll look and feel behind the wheel, but he never allows you to look under the hood. Think Nancy Pelosi's, "We have to pass the bill so that you can find out what's in it." Then, when you take that feel-good car on the road, it rattles, clunks, and takes a dump on the freeway. Socialism is a lemon. It is unsustainable. Take it from those in the know: leaders of a nation that crumbled under socialist policies but began to thrive when rational, strong leaders rolled back said policies.

Socialism is a philosophy of failure, the creed of ignorance, and the gospel of envy. Its inherent virtue is the equal sharing of misery.

—Winston Churchill

The problem with socialism is that you eventually run out of other peoples' money.

—Margaret Thatcher

#Socialism, #SocialismFail, #Leftism

Sortition

Noun

The practice of randomly selecting an officer or politician from a large pool rather than based on merit. Similar to how a jury is selected, it is basically drawing straws. In ancient Athens, the birthplace of democracy, sortition was the primary method of appointing people to political offices based on the belief that it would allow for an indiscriminate representation of the people.

There are still some who believe sortition should replace elections of legislators as a way to root out corruption and ensure fair representation of the interests of the people. Clearly, proponents have never served on jury duty. A day in a jury room exposes every level of intellect, prejudice, character, work ethic, critical thinking skills, and excuse-making abilities.

Thankfully, in the final selection of a jury, prosecutors, defense attorneys, and judges pose questions to uncover whether a person is smart enough to comprehend the basic rule of law. The same must be done when choosing political candidates.

Sortition is a shot in the dark. It's playing with fire. A spin of the roulette wheel, skating on thin ice, and any other idiomatic expression used to describe a fool's errand.

Speaker of the House

Noun

The presiding officer of the U.S. House of Representatives and second in line of succession to the presidency. He or she is chosen by the majority party on the first day of every new Congress. Duties include administering the oath of office to new members, calling the House to order, setting rules on procedures, appointing members to select and conference committees, and determining which committee will consider which bills. The speaker is, literally, the "head of the House."

He or she declares and defends his or her party's legislative agenda. Therefore, the bills the speaker favors get out of committee and come to the floor for a vote much faster than others. As a leader, the speaker is always more high profile than other members, but even more so when the opposing party is in the White House. It is then that the speaker becomes front and center as the "face" of the opposition, taking on a much more prominent role in public debate. Tip O'Neill, Newt Gingrich, and Nancy Pelosi became household (pun intended) names because they were in constant battle with the resident of 1600 Pennsylvania Avenue.

#SpeakerOfTheHouse, #HouseOfReps

Statist

Noun

Someone who believes the state to be of utmost authority, who relies on the state to control the economy and the general public welfare, and therefore defers all power to the state, whenever necessary. (See **Autocracy**.)

Stimulus

Noun

The use of monetary incentive or fiscal policy change to jump-start a downward-trending economy. It is taxpayer money injected into the economy via government loans, grants, bailouts, and infrastructure projects.

In 2009, Barack Obama and the Democrats in Congress passed a stimulus bill that ultimately totaled over $800 billion. They vowed lofty outcomes like millions of new jobs, a drop in unemployment, and a promise that two million people would be magically lifted out of poverty. They promised shovel-ready jobs in infrastructure, but two years later the United States had experienced a drop in infrastructure spending and the Census Bureau reported that 2.6 million people fell *into* poverty. In fact, the nonworking went from 83.3 million to 86.7 million. So much for all those new jobs. Obama then later admitted that shovel-ready jobs didn't really exist.

Unemployment was at 7.8 percent in 2009, and the administration claimed the stimulus would help it drop below 6 percent by 2012. Instead, in that year, it hit 8.1 percent. Why? Because, in truth, stimulus proponents think like President Obama, who said, "What do you think a stimulus is? It's spending—that's the whole point! Seriously."

Yes, Barry, a stimulus *is* spending, but spending is *not* the point. The point is to *stimulate* the economy, that is, encourage growth via wage increases and job creation. It did not do that. At all. Seriously. (See **Bailout** for a list of boondoggles.)

Conversely, by lowering taxes, freeing the economy, and encouraging businesses overseas to return to the United States with incentives, the economy has roared into the new decade under the leadership of President Donald Trump. That's a real stimulus. Unfortunately, with the COVID-19 enforced lockdown, the previously self-stimulated economy has collapsed. Many have postulated that the economic shutdown was an anti-Trump maneuver.

Regardless, a few bucks from the government won't effectively jump-start an engine that has no gas.

> *Every time I hear a politician mention the word "stimulus," my mind flashes back to high school biology class, when I touched battery wires to a dead frog to make it twitch.*
>
> —Robert Kiyosakei, author of *Rich Dad, Poor Dad*

Like the jolt of electricity, a stimulus may cause a "twitch," but it does not bring the economy back to life.

#Stimulus, #DeficitSpending

Straw man argument

Noun

Exaggerating, misrepresenting, or lying about an opponent's point of view in order to easily refute it. A logical fallacy, giving the *illusion* that one is actually debating and destroying the opposition.

President Obama had a closet full of straw men he regularly pulled out and set up so he could knock them down, pretending he'd made salient points. Here are some of his highlights:

> We, the people, still believe that enduring security and lasting peace do not require perpetual war.

His implication is that anyone opposed to his national security views wants an ongoing, everlasting war. But nobody has ever proposed that, nor do they want it. It's easier to paint Republicans as warmongers than to debate any merits of military involvement.

> Apparently, they're scared of widows and orphans coming into the United States of America as part of our tradition of compassion.

Politicians and the public voiced their concerns about insufficient vetting to weed out terrorists among Syrian refugees. But rather than address the issue, Obama called critics callous scaredy cats and accused them of being afraid of harmless innocents.

> It's not surprising, then, they get bitter, they cling to guns or religion or antipathy to people who aren't like them or anti-immigrant sentiment or anti-trade sentiment as a way to explain their frustrations.

Boiling people's authentic arguments down to a choice soundbite for political purposes is the lazy coward's way out. Not to be outdone by the president, minority leader Nancy Pelosi raided a bale of hay to set this guy up after the Supreme Court issued its ruling in *Burell v. Hobby Lobby*.

> We should be afraid of this court, the five guys who start determining what contraceptions are legal.

The court ruled that businesses could decide on religious grounds not to pay for *certain types* (abortion inducing) of contraception. It had nothing to do with the legality of birth control. But Pelosi wants birth control and abortion to be free and on-demand, so she completely ignored that the ruling was about religious liberty and made up an oppositional, strawman, position.

#StrawMan, #RedHerring, #LogicalFallacy

Sunset clause

Noun

A clause attached to a bill or law that ends sections or the entirety of it after a certain date unless action is taken to extend it. A sunset clause is an expiration date and is generally placed on a bill when action is required quickly and the full ramifications of it have not been examined.

A more frequent use of sunset clauses would force Congress to reevaluate the necessity of the regulations or agencies created by certain acts. Also, without a sunset clause forcing a law to expire, special interest groups and politicians may see no reason to change it if they benefit from its current existence. Sunset clauses used in more regularity can help ensure that regulations and laws are justified and necessary.

Swing voter

Noun

Some define a swing voter as someone who votes by thought and not by party lines. Ironically, those defining it that way aren't using much thought. A more accurate description is: a swing voter is someone who votes by feelings, not by philosophies.

There may be individual issues that one may disagree with, but there is a stark line between the two parties. Republicans want small, limited government. Democrats desire a big, controlling state. Republicans champion individual liberty and personal accountability. Democrats attempt to stifle speech and divide people by race, class, and gender. These are very different, contrasting views of the role of government. Swinging back and forth between parties and deciding on personality instead of principles are not thought based.

> *Swing voters are more appropriately known as the "idiot voters" because they have no set of philosophical principles. By the age of fourteen, you're either a Conservative or a Liberal if you have an IQ above a toaster.*
>
> —Ann Coulter

Put another way: you are either for freedom or for slavery. Conservatives seek maximum freedom, while Democrats/leftists love to limit it using government.

#SwingVoter, #SwingState

Syndicalism

Noun

A worker-based movement via unions: organized syndicates. It is opposed to capitalism but also socialism because it seeks to abolish the state, seeing the state as an oppressive enforcer of capitalism.

A combination of Marxism and anarchism, syndicalism has its roots in the late 1800s in France and wove its way through other European nations and the United States (as the Industrial Workers of the World—IWW) in the early part of the 20th century, promoting class warfare. The IWW's goal was the destruction of existing society by overthrowing capitalism. It sought to band together labor unions and strike all industries at the same time. God bless the service workers, tradesman, and factory workers, but they don't employ themselves. Topple the employers, and the workers have no jobs.

Systemic racism

Noun

Also known as "institutional racism," systemic racism is a theory that claims that the system itself, based on its foundation, is racist, that racism is imbedded in the very structure of society—specifically the United States, because apparently no other society deserves the same kind of scrutiny. Why? Because the United States is the most prosperous nation, and the Left, which is the group that touts all the failures of America, seeks only to undermine human advancement and impoverish everyone. But the idea that a system itself can be racist, without any concrete proof of such practices, falls on its face.

The myriad examples of the success stories of the so-called minority underclass is witness to the great opportunities that exist in the United States, which is by-and-large color blind. For a multi-million-dollar-earning athlete to claim systemic racism is absurdity itself. For the president of the United States to further racist stereotypes is hypocrisy. These minorities in leadership have a duty to defend the system that permitted and encouraged their successes, but instead they seek to destroy.

The question that never gets answered is, what will replace this so-called systemic corruption? That answer is simply undefined, because it will be simply different corruption. A society that sacrificed 600,000 souls in a war for equality for all, after fighting the Revolutionary War against the then greatest nation-power on Earth, using the slogan "No Taxation Without Representation" (which was seen as a different form of slavery), ought to be afforded due credit. But, as an enemy of human prosperity, the Left always seeks to condemn and destroy, now with the absurd claim of systemic racism. By way of proof, they say it is so ingrained one can't even see it. Like a microaggression, that you can't even feel, the racism exists, though there is no evidence.

But isn't that their same argument *against* the existence of God? If you can't actually see it, it doesn't exist, right?

No, the term has become simply a catch-all to imply guilt for success. Any advancement, even if made by a minority, must be abandoned because of its genesis in a racist system! It's a pejorative intended to silence discussion and control.

It really has no meaning that can be specified and tested in the way that one tests hypotheses.

—Thomas Sowell on systemic racism

Tea Party

Noun

A conservative movement born out of protests against the federal government. On February 19, 2009, business pundit Rick Santelli ranted on CNBC against the irresponsible government bailouts that would benefit those who deserved it least, using the finances of those who acted most responsibly. Santelli, seemingly off the cuff, invited conservatives to join him for a "tea party" in Chicago that July. The Tea Party exploded to millions by April 15, 2009, with over 800 protests across the country. It has since become a major political force seeking to reduce the size and reach of the federal government and return to the core principle of the nation: freedom. The name is inspired from the Boston Tea Party of 1773 that kicked off the Revolutionary War, when the colonial settlers decided to protest the unfair British tax on tea.

Liberals like to claim that the Tea Party is an extremist, racist organization, but their rallies call for electing true conservatives to cut spending, balance the budget, and return the power to the people. Unlike Black Lives Matter, which incites violence by shouting, "What do we want? Dead cops!" and, again in reference to the police, "Pigs in a blanket, fry 'em like bacon," the Tea Party presses to audit the IRS and repeal Obamacare via violence-free legislation. Opponents condemn the Tea Party's cucumber sandwiches while simultaneously tossing Molotov cocktails.

> *I have a message from the Tea Party, a message that is loud and clear and does not mince words. We've come to take our government back.*
>
> —Rand Paul

#TeaParty, #Tcot, #LimitedGovernment

TERF

Noun

This acronym stands for Trans-Exclusionary Radical Feminist and originated in 2008 to refer to staunch feminists who asserted that there is something special about being female. Famed author J. K. Rowling was labeled a "hater" for insinuating that *only* "people who menstruate" (as referred to in an article she tweeted) should be called *women*. (How *dare* she?) The trans community found this characterization troubling because it necessarily precluded men from establishing their personal womanhood.

That's kind of the point, though, isn't it? A feminist should seek to uphold the female (yes, we know, in reality, many of them don't). Preserving and promoting the female necessarily disallow transgressions against it, or it dissolves in a sea of sameness. But, of course, the trans community sees honest feminists as a threat, thus the invented nasty-sounding label! Name calling is very effective in a culture of "likes."

With this new word, it's easy to negatively label anyone who questions the idea of men competing in women's sports (and winning handily), even though Title 9 sports was something feminists valiantly fought for.

> *If sex isn't real, there's no same-sex attraction. If sex isn't real, the lived reality of women globally is erased. . . . erasing the concept of sex removes the ability of many to meaningfully discuss their lives. It isn't hate to speak the truth.*
>
> —J. K. Rowling

Terrorism

Noun

The use of intimidation, fear, and violence in pursuit of a political aim. Terrorism is employed by a number of ideologies: eco-terrorists, Spain's Basque separatists, Northern Ireland's, IRA, and Columbia's FARC. But Islamic radicalism is by far the most chronic, growing, and murderous embodiment of terrorism.

Terrorists intimidate through fear. But if terrorists simply wanted to scare us, they'd jump out of a closet and shout "Boo." Instead, they fly airplanes into buildings, bomb a marathon, attack a consulate in Benghazi, and shoot up a publisher's office and a concert theater in Paris. Islamic terrorism murders with the goal of destroying Western civilization and ruling with Sharia law.

Speaking of the Left, Andrew McCarthy said:

In their minds, violence has nothing to do with Islam . . . and the fact that Muslims are committing it is happenstance. There's no doctrinal underpinning to it. . . . That's why you see them so hesitant to say what's obviously terrorism is terrorism.

There can be no parsing of words, no rationalization of motives, nor fear of offending, when it comes to discussion of terrorism.

One does not need to be an official member of al-Qaeda or ISIS to be a terrorist. An American Islamic extremist shouting "Allahu Akbar" while shooting up an army base is *not* workplace violence; it is terrorism. These heinous acts are no longer confined to the centralized groups in a far-off land; they are here, in America. ISIS, Hamas, Hezbollah, Boko Haram, al-Qaeda, Taliban, and so on have emboldened an increasing number of factions, affiliates, and "lone wolves" that may not have the leadership or particular group identity but are deadly just the same.

#KeepAmericaSafe, #Terrorism

Theocracy

Noun

A system of government ruled by priests claiming divine authority. The term means "rule of God" and comes from the Greek *theos* ("God") and *kratia* ("power or strength").

Iran is a theocracy. Although it has an elected president, a legislature, and a judiciary, ultimate control rests in the hands of the Supreme Leader. He sets the tone of domestic and foreign policies, is the commander-in-chief of the military and the sole person to declare war, is head of intelligence, can appoint and dismiss members of the judiciary and media outlets, and appoints half the members of the Council of Guardians that oversees Parliament. He is the highest-ranking official in the country and exerts his power with the more than 2,000 clerics he authorizes to intervene in any matters of state.

Civil law is imposed by religious dictate and interpreted by religious courts. There is no separation of church and state in a theocracy.

#Theocracy, #Iran, #SupremeLeader

Think tank

Noun

Key persons of influence brainstorming, as a group, to solve a particular economic, social, or political issue. It is a foundation or institute designed to perform research, analysis, and advocacy on topics such as the economy, immigration, the military, foreign policy, and the environment, among others. Most are nonprofit, funded by private and corporate donors. Some are ideologically driven, while others are issue focused.

#HeritageFoundation, #HooverInstitute, #AmericanEnterpriseInstitute

Totalitarianism

Noun

A system of government with absolute, total control over all elements of civilians' lives. North Korea, Cuba, and the former Soviet Union are examples of totalitarian states where citizens cannot choose where they live, cannot freely practice their chosen religion, cannot travel abroad, and cannot join or form nongovernment organizations. The economy is centrally planned (poorly), so most live in poverty, and all media are operated by the government to ensure statist propaganda. Education is strictly controlled in order to indoctrinate children to accept the ideology. Information from outside sources, such as foreign media or the Internet, is extremely limited, lest the people get a taste of freedom. To speak against the regime is a crime punishable by imprisonment, forced labor, torture, and even death.

Totalitarianism views have gained momentum in America as the Left demands conformity in thought, speech, and belief. President Obama declared the science settled on climate change—who knew former community experts were scientific experts? In traditional totalitarian fashion, the *Los Angeles Times* currently refrains from publishing letters with contrary viewpoints.

Bakeries who disagree with same-sex marriage are forced to participate in them or suffer public disgrace and economic ruin. The Left has invaded personal habits, activities, and even homes: some cities have outlawed smoking on public streets, hurled dodgeball from schools, and flicked incandescent lightbulbs out of commission. Dissent is deemed racist, sexist, or bigoted, and the dissenter is branded as vile. Kim Jong Un couldn't be prouder.

> *The left is entering a new phase of ideological agitation—no longer trying to win the debate but stopping debate altogether, banishing from public discourse any and all opposition. The proper word for that attitude is totalitarian.*
>
> —Charles Krauthammer

#Totalitarianism, #Totalitarian, #BannedSpeech

Transportation Security Administration (TSA)

Noun

An agency of the Department of Homeland Security that governs public travel spaces in the United States. Created in response to the September 11, 2011, terrorist attacks, it replaced private companies with a federally centralized organization to oversee security for highways, trains and mass transit, ports, and especially air travel.

Like most federal agencies, the TSA is too big and too politically correct to be effective. It employs a one-size-fits-all approach, treating all travelers as if they are potential threats. The result has been shoeless travelers waiting in extremely long lines to get patted down and frequently groped, according to the numerous sexual misconduct allegations. Helpless Midwestern grannies and towheaded toddlers are not above suspicion because to focus on a specific profile would be racist.

Widely criticized is the effectiveness of the multitude of checks and regulations, and rightly so. An internal investigation reported severe gaps in security procedure, revealing that banned items were able to get through security 95 percent of the time. Standard procedures also failed to identify 73 terrorism-affiliated aviation workers. If you can't beat the terrorists, hire 'em?

#TSA, #DHS

Trojan horse

Noun

A hollow, wooden structure created by the Greeks as a disguise to secret their soldiers into Troy. After tricking the Trojans into admitting this gift inside the city walls, the soldiers leapt out, let their fellow warriors in, and destroyed the city.

Candidate Barack Obama in 2008 was a Trojan horse. Painted as a moderate unifier seeking to end partisanship and heal the wounds of racial discrimination as America's first black president

(Bill Clinton's claims notwithstanding), he was presented to the American people as an agent of "hope and change" to calm the strife and save the nation from itself. But when wheeled into the White House, out popped the warriors against freedom—encouraging onerous regulations, federal overreach, and race baiting.

Often the true intent of proposals, bills, and executive actions are hidden in the belly of the horse. Many called the Federal Communication Commission's net neutrality rules a Trojan horse. Trumpeted as a means to create more Internet freedom by prohibiting Internet service providers from charging content producers more for speedier access, in reality, it was the government warrior agents intervening to seize control of private enterprise.

Trump Day

Noun

Synonym for "hump day," which refers to Wednesday—the halfway point of the work week. Originally brought into focus by radio talk host Ken Matthews, but let's face it, for Trump's staunch supporters, every day is Trump Day—a cause of celebration because Hillary isn't president.

Trump effect

Noun

An awakening to a new reverence for freedom and strength as a nation, pride in true progress. A phenomenon in business, but even more so in politics, Donald J. Trump was elected president of the United States in 2016. In a well-known interview with Oprah decades before, Trump expressed only mild interest in running for president but predicted that if he did, he would win. Against all odds (and Hillary Clinton with puppet-master George Soros), he did prevail, and many saw that as God's protection of the United States. Trump ran a campaign about making America great again, or MAGA. Leftists claimed that America was never great and that it was racist to suggest such a thing. And they wonder how that mantra doesn't win.

Since Trump's election, nations around the world have followed suit with their own versions of him. Hungary, Austria, Brazil, and England—with Boris Johnson (BoJo)—have all implemented pro-national policies and controlled or curtailed immigration policies. BoJo is engaged in withdrawing the boot of the European Union socialists from the neck of Britain via Brexit. Polls predicted that Brexit would fail miserably, and leftists cried and predicted the end of the world when it won handily. They were all confused, because none of them knew anyone who would vote for individual sovereignty—the right to determine one's own way in the world—which is what Brexit represented.

Similarly, polls erroneously predicted that Hillary would win. Though Trump's ascendance to the presidency came after Brexit's overwhelming victory, we can safely say that his appearance has bolstered the defiance of the statists' control worldwide.

#TrumpEffect, #Trump, #MAGA

Unemployment rate

Noun

The number of unemployed individuals as a percentage of the labor force.

Although a low unemployment rate can be an indicator of economic health, it cannot be taken at face value as a precise representation of how many are truly unemployed. The number is drawn from Bureau of Labor Statistics surveys that count *any* work for pay during the survey week as employment. If a person worked for a friend organizing paperwork for one day, the government counts him or her employed. The unemployment rate does not include the people who have stopped looking for work altogether, and there are many people only working part-time who desire full-time employment. For a true picture of the workforce participation, other factors must be considered, and comparing the rate to previous years can also prove useful.

#UnemploymentRate, #ParticipationRate

UBI or universal basic income

Noun

In principle, an unconditional baseline salary to ensure citizens of a minimum standard of living, a guaranteed safety net. But, in reality, it's a pipe dream, generated in part by legalizing marijuana. Cost of living in New York City or San Francisco is much higher than in Springfield, so, in a country of tremendous diversity, how would one determine appropriate values?

UBI has been embraced by the fringes of both sides of the political spectrum. Some say it focuses too much on wealth (or lack thereof), while others insist it would encourage a "something for nothing" type of entitlement mentality—which, of course, it would. We prefer the tried and true *Give a man a fish, and you feed him for a day; teach a man to fish, and you feed him for a lifetime.*

The Finnish theory behind UBI is to afford people the freedom to acquire new skills or develop new talents for the marketplace. The Finns tried it for unemployed folks, and surprisingly, while participants reportedly felt happier overall, those people ended up not procuring employment. Shocker, right?

The real issue with just giving away cash is that it devalues the cash. It seems few have studied the inflating effects of Dire Straits' "Money for Nothing" strategy.

> *I'm a capitalist, and I believe that universal basic income is necessary for capitalism to continue.*
>
> —Andrew Yang, 2020 Democratic presidential candidate

Useful idiot (Nancy Pelosi)

Noun

A tool in a political scheme to fool the public. The term is attributed to Vladimir Lenin describing soft-hearted supporters who excused the actions of communist Soviet Union.

Dictators of the world love the useful idiots of the West. During Fidel Castro's takeover of Cuba, dreamy-eyed sympathizers bought his promises of liberation and freedom hook, line, and sinker. He never held a free election but established a police state and jailed or executed all opposition. His useful idiots defended the cause, asserting that people can choose the political systems and lifestyles they want. Because they're idiots, they completely overlooked the fact that the people did *not* choose it.

Useful idiots are often found among the intelligentsia/elite, caught up in a fact-absent fairyland promoting very dangerous ideas. Professors and students chanting for speech codes are actually petitioning to hand their futures to a controlling state. President Obama embarked on apology tours after taking office, traveling to foreign nations and virtually prostrating the United States at their feet. Humiliating America while excusing the Islamic world's terror campaigns and China's human rights violations are signatures on our own death warrants.

#UsefulIdiots, #Elites

Utilitarianism

Noun

A theory that actions are right only if in the best interest of the greater good. It denies intrinsic right and wrong. Thus, good and evil are irrelevant. Value depends only on the utility of the consequences of the nonmoral goods, such as pleasure, happiness, satisfaction, or supposed benefit to society.

Adopting this view clearly eliminates morality. For example, care for the disabled or terminally ill elderly incurs a great investment of time, effort, and finances. The utilitarian view justifies withholding care or even murder because it seeks simply to minimize costs. It defends a mother's "choice" to abort by virtue of convenience. The "death panels" of Obamacare would have made utilitarian decisions regarding the financial apportionment of care. Utilitarianism fails to consider individual gifts and less obvious abilities. Stephen Hawking was a phenomenal theoretical physicist that utilitarianism would have prescribed eliminating.

The idea that worth be based only on the greatest happiness for the greatest number of people begs some questions. Who determines happiness? Who is the benevolent oracle who decides this so-called greater good? Slavery financially benefited society, so why did we abolish it? Oh, that's right, it was immoral.

#Utilitarianism, #Relativism

Veteran

Noun

A person who has served in the military and put duty and honor to the country above personal safety. A man or woman who knew the risks and dangers of war but was willing to step in harm's way to defend the values of the nation.

On one day in November we recognize and honor the service of veterans. Rather paltry, given they protect our freedom *every* day of the year.

> *We owe our World War II veterans—and all our veterans—a debt we can never fully repay.*
>
> —Doc Hastings

#Veterans, #Vets, #VetsRising

Vice president

Noun

The presidential running mate and occasional stand-in for the president, empowered to assume the duties on the presidency in the case of death, disability, or absence.

Comedian Conan O'Brien joked, "A high school girl has invited Joe Biden to be her prom date. Isn't that nice? However, her father is refusing to let her go with a guy who can't really describe what he does for a living." The quote has only become more ironic, given Biden's mental state during the 2020 presidential campaign.

Seriously, what does that guy roaming the East Wing, the first in line of succession to Barack Obama, actually do? His primary role is to be available to be president if necessary. His secondary duty is as president of the Senate, where he rarely participates except to break a tie. Franklin Roosevelt's first vice president, John Nance Garner, declared the position "a no man's land somewhere between the legislative and executive branch." He also reportedly commented that it wasn't "worth a bucket of warm spit." He said it, not me.

The VP's extent of involvement is usually dependent upon his or her relationship with the president. And although the president chooses his VP, often it's for electoral purposes and not because he or she respects or gets along with him or her.

Some VPs do, in fact, perform executive functions. Richard Nixon, under Eisenhower, attended hundreds of Cabinet and National Security Council sessions. Mike Pence, under Donald Trump, brilliantly headed up the taskforce to deal with the Wuhan coronavirus.

Prior to the passage of the 12th Amendment, the vice president was the runner-up in the presidential election. John Adams was not George Washington's running mate; he was his competition.

War

Noun

Throughout history, many have offered views on war. Roman statesman/scholar/writer Cicero defined it as "a contention by force," and Thomas Hobbes believed war was beyond the act of fighting: "By war is meant a state of affairs, which may exist even while its operations are not continued."

There are a number of reasons for war: power, territory, resources, ideals, or a combination of some or all. It is ugly, it is brutal, and it is hell, but sometimes it is necessary and just. (See **Jus ad bellum**.)

As stated in Article 1, Section 2, Clause 11, of the Constitution, for the United States to be technically "at war," it must be declared by Congress. But when jihadists spanning numerous countries are actively assaulting and killing Americans, "technically" goes out the window. War goes beyond a declaration. It is a battle of ideologies and, for the United States, a fight to preserve liberty. As much as Obama would like, he cannot proclaim that a war is over if the enemy is still fighting. Romantic pacifists and isolationists who believe that we can "make love, not war," roll up the carpet, and sing folk songs, would do well to remember what Russian revolutionary Leon Trotsky said, "You may not be interested in war, but war is interested in you."

#War, #DefendAmerica, #DefeatRadicalIslam

Wealth

Noun

Affluence or abundance. The possession of valuable material or resources.

Wealth is created in the free exchange of goods, whereby each participant trades something of lesser value to them for something of greater value. Each party leaves the exchange *wealthier*.

The Seven Social Sins are

Wealth without work.
Pleasure without conscience.
Knowledge without character.
Commerce without morality.
Science without humanity.
Worship without sacrifice.
Politics without principle.

—Frederick Lewis Donaldson, priest, minister

Weather underground

Organization

A radical Left militant organization that sought to advance communism through violent revolution, including bombings, in the 1960s and 1970s. Founded in part by Bill Ayers, who is credited with giving President Obama his start in politics and who then became a "distinguished professor" at the University of Illinois. Membership included Bernardine Dohrn, a convicted domestic terrorist and currently an associate professor of law at Northwestern University.

#terrorism

Whip

Noun

The member in his or her party in the legislature responsible for wrangling and counting votes before a bill comes up for an official vote. Their job is to "whip" up the votes by "whipping" the party members into line.

Think of Congress as the mafia: the majority leader is the Godfather, and the whip is the wise guy muscle.

White privilege

Noun

The societal benefits generated by Western culture, widely attributed to the Caucasian race in Europe and the Americas. The idea that being white affords generalized advantages, despite perhaps the white person coming from the same socioeconomic strata of society as many other colors. White privilege is seen as having roots in European colonialism, mainly because those words have become the repository of all negativity, despite the tremendous strides in prosperity gained by this terrible Western culture.

White privilege is used to provoke white guilt, which can be easily exploited for personal gain.

In a conversation about race, Oprah Winfrey said:

> There are white people who are not as powerful as the system of white people—the caste system that's been put in place. But they still, no matter where they are on the rung or ladder of success, they still have their whiteness.

Many remarked on the intrinsic racism in her comment, while others derided her hypocrisy—she's worth an immense $2.6 billion.

Ultimately, what is meant by white privilege is really "green privilege," or wealth. The phrase effectively abdicates responsibility.

Claiming that some people "luck into" prosperity by virtue of their skin color allows proponents to justify their envy and resentment and more easily accept their own failures. It is the basket of excuses for people who give up.

> CNN legal analyst Areva Martin: "That's a whole, other long conversation about white privilege, the things that you have the privilege of doing, that people of color don't have the privilege of."
>
> Radio and Fox Nation host David Webb: "How do I have the privilege of white privilege?"
>
> Martin: "David, by virtue of being a white male you have white privilege."
>
> Webb: "I hate to break it to you, but you should've been better prepped. I'm black."

There is no such thing as white privilege.

—David Webb

Woke

Adjective

A term to describe someone who understands racial and social justice issues or generally embraces new cultural norms as imposed by the Left. After the Trayvon Martin shooting in 2012, the nascent Black Lives Matter movement promoted #staywoke and then revived it more during their climb in power. Really, it's just a way to positively spin the destruction of Western culture before our eyes.

More recently, the word has morphed into a pejorative! Now UrbanDictionary.com defines it as "The act of being very pretentious about how much you care about a social issue."

If you want to be woke, do so at your own peril.

Wonk

Noun

A person who takes excessive interest in minor details of political policy. Wonks revel in the macro, micro, and minutiae of bills, processes, and proceedings. Appropriation, markup, quorum, and cloture are regular parts of their vernacular. Mention one of them, and it can send them into a fit of enthusiasm known as "wonking out." Technology has its nerds; politics has its wonks.

#Wonk, #PolicyWonk

Xenophobia

Noun

From the Greek *xénos* which means "foreigner or stranger," xenophobia refers to the fear of anything foreign or unfamiliar. Today, it is used as a pejorative for people who support nationalism or show signs of patriotism. It is used as a bullying weapon to intimidate citizens to accept foreign ideas or people via intimidation.

Wikipedia holds that xenophobes may fear loss of racial identity, which proves the lie behind our racial politics. How can one lose one's racial identity via foreign interference?

Xenophobia indicates a fear of the novel. A better approach is an adherence to traditional values with an openness for improvements. It's admittedly a delicate balance, but one that can be achieved, for instance, by President Trump. Instead, the Left uses xenophobia as a sledge hammer to bludgeon anyone with conservative leanings and anything from traditional Western culture, also. That's why it has become synonymous with America; it's intended to destroy our borders.

> *The pandemic has unleashed familiar forces of hate, fear and xenophobia that he always flames . . . that have always existed in this society.*
>
> —Joe Biden, about the Trump response to COVID-19

Zeitgeist

Noun

A German word translated to mean "time-ghost" or "spirit of the age." It can be used in a targeted way to describe trends in entertainment, technology, and culture. But those trends are generally representative of society's overall zeitgeist of intellectual and moral consensus.

The current zeitgeist is postmodernism, marked by subjectivism and moral relativism. It contends that morals are not absolute. Postmodernism refuses to accept a transcendent fixed idea of right and wrong or good and evil. This era of self-focus, instant gratification, and no accountability is our zeitgeist.

The truth often combats the zeitgeist. The world does not owe you. Speak *the* (not *your*) truth, always.

#Zeitgeist, #Trending, #MoralRelativism

APPENDIX A

Alinksy's 12 Rules on "Power Tactics"

1. "Power is not only what you have, but what the enemy thinks you have." Power is derived from two main sources—money and people. "Have-nots" must build power from flesh and blood.

2. "Never go outside the expertise of your people." It results in confusion, fear, and retreat. Feeling secure adds to the backbone of anyone.

3. "Whenever possible, go outside the expertise of the enemy." Look for ways to increase insecurity, anxiety, and uncertainty.

4. "Make the enemy live up to its own book of rules." If the rule is that every letter gets a reply, send 30,000 letters. You can kill them with this because no one can possibly obey all of their own rules.

5. "Ridicule is man's most potent weapon." There is no defense. It's irrational. It's infuriating. It also works as a key pressure point to force the enemy into concessions.

6. "A good tactic is one your people enjoy." They'll keep doing it without urging and come back to do more. They're doing their thing and will even suggest better ones.

7. "A tactic that drags on too long becomes a drag." Don't become old news.

8. "Keep the pressure on. Never let up." Keep trying new things to keep the opposition off balance. As the opposition masters one approach, hit them from the flank with something new.

9. "The threat is usually more terrifying than the thing itself." Imagination and ego can dream up many more consequences than any activist.

10. "If you push a negative hard enough, it will push through and become a positive." Violence from the other side can win the public to your side because the public sympathizes with the underdog.

11. "The price of a successful attack is a constructive alternative." Never let the enemy score points because you're caught without a solution to a problem.

12. "Pick the target, freeze it, personalize it, and polarize it." Cut off the support network and isolate the target from sympathy. Go after people and not institutions; people hurt faster than institutions.

Adapted from *Rules for Radicals: A Practical Primer for Realistic Radicals* by Saul D. Alinsky, Random House, 1971.

APPENDIX B

A Summary of the U.S. Bill of Rights

1. Congress shall make no law respecting an establishment of religion, or prohibiting the free exercise thereof; or abridging the freedom of speech, or of the press, or the right of the people peaceably to assemble, and to petition the government for a redress of grievances.

2. The right of the people to keep and bear arms shall not be infringed.

3. No soldier shall be quartered in any house without the consent of the owner.

4. The right of the people to be secure in their persons, houses, papers, and effects, against unreasonable search and seizures, shall not be violated.

5. No person shall be subject for the same offense to be twice put in jeopardy of life or limb, nor shall be compelled in any criminal case to be a witness against himself.

6. In all criminal prosecutions, the accused shall enjoy the right to a speedy and public trial; to be confronted with the witnesses against him; to have compulsory process for obtaining witnesses in his favor, and to have the assistance of counsel for his defense.

7. The right of a trial by jury shall be preserved.

8. Excessive bail shall not be required, nor excessive fines imposed, nor cruel and unusual punishments inflicted (full text).

9. The enumeration in the Constitution of certain rights shall not be construed to deny or disparage others retained by the people (full text).

10. The powers not delegated to the United States by the Constitution, nor prohibited by it to the states, are reserved to the states respectively, or to the people (full text).

Acknowledgments

I'd like to acknowledge the tremendous support of my radio listeners and Twitter followers, who put up with (and even support) my nerdy obsession with language and my mom-puns. I must also thank my long-suffering husband and children, who patiently listened to my complaints about the abuse of grammar that runs rampant in the national discussion, often answering with, "What?" Finally, I'm so grateful to Mary Glenn and Keith Pfeffer at Humanix and Christopher Ruddy at Newsmax for understanding importance of our words and appreciating the value of this little book.

About the Author

A native of Pittsburgh, Pennsylvania, Sam Sorbo attended Duke University before opting to travel the world pursuing a successful international fashion modeling career. This led to acting work. Sam performed in many films, like *Bonfire of the Vanities* and *Twenty Bucks*, and television, including *Jag* and *Chicago Hope*, before guest starring on *Hercules*, when Kevin Sorbo swept her off her feet. They married  in 1998. Kevin suffered three strokes prior to their wedding, which prompted Sam to step back from her active career and tend to him instead.

Several years, two boys, and a girl later, Sam became an unlikely but impassioned advocate for home education. She wrote *They're YOUR Kids: My Journey from Self-Doubter to Home School Advocate* (Reveille Press) to empower parents to reimagine their children's education standards and accept the responsibility, challenge, and immeasurable joy of personally teaching their own offspring. Her next book, *Teach from Love* (Broadstreet), is a school-year devotional for families that focuses on instilling godly virtues in our children. Of course, Kevin and Sam home educate their three children.

While she continues acting, producing, and writing, as well as hosting the daily *Sam Sorbo Show* radio show, Sam is a sought-after public speaker, and she enjoys engaging her audiences in a new national dialog about how we define education as a nation and a culture.

Together, the Sorbos produced and starred in the surprise hit movie *Let There Be Light,* which Sam wrote, Kevin directed, and Sean Hannity executive produced. The film, which featured Dionne Warwick, Travis Tritt, and the Sorbo boys Braeden and Shane, highlighted faith, family, and forgiveness. The Sorbos' new film, *Miracle in East Texas: A Tall Tale Inspired by an Absolutely True Story,* is a romantic comedy about two con men and the biggest oil strike in history. With their Sorbo Family Film Studios, they seek to elevate Christian values, inspire hope, and restore the Judeo-Christian American culture.

Contact: SamSorbo.com
Twitter: @TheSamSorbo
FB: The Official Sam Sorbo Page
Insta: Sam_Sorbo